LET THAT SHIT GO

A Journey to Forgiveness,

Healing & Understanding Love

BRUNA NESSIF

of The Problem With Dating

I

Dedicated to you.

May you always find the courage to feel,

forgive, heal & love unconditionally.

TABLE OF CONTENTS

"You own everything that happened to you. Tell your stories. If people wanted you to write warmly about them, they should have behaved better."

-**Anne Lamott,** *Bird by Bird: Some Instructions on Writing and Life*

Sigh,

Let it go, they said. It's easy, they said. *Yeah, OK.*

If letting go was easy, we'd all do it effortlessly and never have to deal with the shit that comes our way when we don't. But, that's not usually the case, is it?

Have you ever let your mind wander on a topic, so much so that you begin to question absolutely everything? You analyze, you observe, you come up with possible outcomes and theories, and then when you share these thoughts with someone else, they come back at your thorough investigation findings with, "It's not that deep"?

Ever since I was a young girl, I was always curious. I must have had dozens of those random question-and-answer books, because I wanted to know anything I could about everything. Why is the sky blue? How do birds fly? Who came up with the days of the week? How deep is the ocean? What happens when we die?

You name it, I asked it. You can imagine how exhausting that was for my parents.

That desire to always dig deeper led me to life-changing discoveries as well as great disappointment as a young adult. While I uncovered meaningful experiences and truths, I was also met with the unfavorable conclusion that the actual meaning behind many of our commonly asked questions were so often covered up in bullshit that many lost the vigor to uncover the root of what's *really* going on—especially when it came to our feelings. It's odd. When you were growing up, it seemed so simple—*I feel sad. I feel happy.* Whatever you were feeling, you voiced fearlessly. When did that start to disappear?

I credit my passionate curiosity for my decision to initially major in Psychology. I really wanted to understand people. I really wanted to understand myself. I wanted to know why we act the way we do, why we say the things we say, and why we react to certain scenarios differently than others.

While that academic road was a short one—because one NeuroPsych class my freshman year of college intimidated me so much that I switched majors—the root of my interest on the matter never went away, hence why we're here.

One of my passions is people. Whether it's the ongoing mystery of figuring out who someone is at their core, myself included, or the realization that I will never fully have the answers on why people do the things they do, I just can't seem to stop myself from at least trying to get as close as I can to solving the riddle that is human nature.

My other passion is love. I'm a lover, what can I say? And when you mix these two things, people and love, you get fascinating results.

It didn't take long for me to realize that love and logic don't always go hand-in-hand. I use myself as an example. From the minute my heart skipped a beat over a boy, my brain seemed to lose some cells and become slightly irrational. OK, maybe a little more than slightly.

The age-old question of, "Do you follow your head or your heart?" gives us this limiting belief from the beginning that these two cannot coexist, because they are not fighting on the same side. We're always fed this notion that you're either logical or you're emotional, but you can't be both.

I wanted to be both, and more.

Combine my curiosity with a passion for people and love, and you're left with a young girl whose mind is like a Google browser with never-ending tabs open all at once, constantly filling up with questions that never seem to get answered, because more often than not, the answers are completely elusive.

Luckily, I had my writing.

Writing is my safe place. I'd jot down whatever came to mind, whether it was a question or just a thought, and put it away. It was a friendship built on scribbled secrets.

As I got older, it became my outlet to express the emotions I was too young to understand. Just picture an only child suffering from that awful, teenage *no-one-ever-understands-me* angst ferociously embedding pages with dark black ink while lying on her bed late at night, and that was basically my adolescence in a nutshell.

Interestingly enough, however, I still do that now. The only difference is I type most of these words down and share them with you (and hopefully, my words are a lot wiser than they were at 15).

And with that, you have Bruna. A passionately curious soul who never gets tired of learning about people's behavior, beginning with herself and her numerous failed attempts at finding "the one," just to ultimately end up on a journey she never realized she needed to be on.

So, you know what? Maybe it *is* that deep.

We've become conditioned to accept superficial conclusions to personal matters, and that's unfortunate, because we'll never heal without the courage to face our wounds with honesty and accountability. Too many people are afraid of letting their minds wander into the depths of their soul because they're afraid of what they might find there, and rightfully so. It's not always pleasant, but blissful ignorance is much worse.

Luckily, you are not one of those people. You know how I know that? Because you picked up this book. Whether you got here in hopes of finding the answers you so desperately seek or just to hear someone else's story, I'm willing to bet that you'll finish with more than you bargained for.

In the decade-plus years of writing about my personal experiences, one thing has been certain—I am not alone in my struggle. If that is true for me, then it is true for you. Emotional wars can feel very isolating, but the truth is many of us are fighting the same battles silently, and because we fight behind closed doors, we become blind to the collective experience, which can provide much needed peace.

As I constantly try to peel off another layer until I get to the very root of who I am, and why I do the things I do, something greater than me, and greater than my fears, continues to tell me that I need to share my journey. Because along with realizing the importance of learning the lesson, I also became very aware of the fact that if I don't learn how to let go, I become paralyzed by everything weighing me down.

Now, I don't know about you, but ain't nobody got time to stay stagnant over here. When you realize that you, and only you, are the reason that your life may or may not be unfolding the way you'd hoped, you begin to do what initially felt impossible.

Like, forgiving someone you trusted for betraying you, learning to love the ugliest parts of yourself, letting go of everything that didn't pan out the way you thought it would, and you start to see that in order to let all that shit go, you first have to give yourself permission to break away from the story you created.

After launching my website The Problem With Dating in 2013, the most common question I'd get asked was—drum roll, please—"What's the problem with dating?" Fair question, obviously, but that was tough to answer, because, sure, we could vent about dating apps, the boom of the digital age, the lack of courting, so on and so forth, but that still wouldn't solve the problem with dating.

That's because the root of the problem with dating is a problem with people. And maybe, if you're anything like me, you begin to wonder if you're a part of that problem, too.

So, as you flip through the pages of this book, consider you are opening the door into my mind and my heart as I reminisce on my story of love lost, my struggle with self-worth, my attempt to understand why my experiences unfolded the way they did and my tumultuous lessons on letting go through the power of forgiveness.

There is one villain and one hero in this story—me.

And so we begin...

1

THE ONE WHO PUSHED ME AWAY

THEY SAY WHEN YOU KNOW, YOU KNOW.

SO WHEN I SAW YOU I KNEW.

MY HEART WAS GOING TO BREAK BECAUSE OF YOU.

STILL, I JUMPED IN.

CALL IT RECKLESS ABANDON.

I JUST NEEDED TO FEEL SOMETHING

AND NOW I CAN'T REMEMBER HOW TO GET BACK
AGAIN.

Here is a constant (and unfortunate) theme with all of my romantic endeavors—I always knew better. I just wouldn't listen.

His smile was my kryptonite, and the moment I saw it, I knew I was in for something I may not come out of unharmed. But that never stopped me, so I dove in, anyway.

It started out just like any other night. My girlfriend Lauren and I got all dolled up to go to the local bars in Pasadena, Calif. We had each recently broken up with our boyfriends (who were brothers), and decided that drowning our failed long-term relationships in some kamikaze shots would become our ultimate method of coping. I threw on my form-fitting little black dress with electric blue pumps, which sounds horrendous now that I think about it, but that was the move at the time. She slipped into a nude strapless mini, and we were off to sip our problems away as we often did.

We hit the usual bars along the strip, before entering the larger, more "clubby" establishment Ménage for some dance relief. While standing at the bar waiting for our liquid poison, we decided to take a selfie. Mind you, this was before selfies were a thing, and I had a Blackberry Storm at the time, so the struggle was real. Every photo was coming out tragic, and during one of my outbursts of laughter at our failure to look sexy, I did a quick scan across the room. That's when my eyes met his. He was already looking at me, and I looked away quickly, because he was too handsome, and I could already feel myself getting flustered. But before I knew it, he was right behind us.

"Do you ladies want me to take the picture for you?"

Oh, he felt sorry for us. Well, at least he was willing to help.

"Sure," I said, and handed him my phone. As Lauren and I began to ease into our stance for the photo, I straightened out my dress, and looked up at him to mouth, "Do I look OK?" He smiled the smile that I would dream about for years, and nodded. He took our picture, walked up to return my phone, and introduced himself.

We exchanged names and he shared that he worked at the venue (nice, I thought, now I know where to find you again), and after thanking him for saving us from our selfie struggle, we went back to drinking at the bar, and he went back to work. Although I could've stayed there, stealing glances at this tall-dark-and-handsome drink of water all night, Lauren and I decided to ditch the spot and go back to one of our favorite bars, Liv, for another round. At this point, the liquor started to hit me, and perhaps that was what gave me the courage to do what I did next.

"We have to go back," I told her.

"Back where?" she asked.

"We have to go back to that bar and I need to ask him if he has a girlfriend."

Lauren, who was no stranger to my forward behavior, couldn't help but raise an eyebrow at my bravado. Whether it was intrigue in what could happen or just the alcohol making her too weak to fight me on this, she obliged. We made the trek back to his venue, and once I got to the door, I asked for him. He popped out from behind the crowd and greeted me with those dimples that I was already lost in.

"Hey!" he excitedly said. I stepped in, stood directly across from him, looked up into his brown eyes and said, "Do you have a girlfriend?"

He smiled, at what I can only assume was his surprise that this short girl had such a big personality, and shook his head.

I was shocked, in all honesty. Here, before me, stood a man who resembled a Greek god, and he was single? I don't know if it was the vodka or just the fact that I knew this moment was a rare one, but I managed to ask, "Can I have your number?"

He answered me with his pearly whites as we exchanged numbers on our phones. We engaged in small talk, yelling over the EDM music about our college experiences and hometowns, and I couldn't tell if it was the butterflies in my stomach or just hunger, but I was feeling something.

Since I wasn't ready to decipher what emotions were already fluttering for this man who I just met but desperately wanted to know, I decided to turn to King Taco to cap the night (tacos are much easier to handle than beautiful men). He texted me as soon as he was off work that night, and we sparked a conversation that lasted for hours, full of all the simple questions many of us ask someone we just met to get a feel for who they are, and that theme continued throughout the week.

The following weekend, I returned to Old Town Pasadena with a coworker of mine after previous plans fell through, and to my delight, he'd found me walking down the street and asked me to come by the bar. One of the things I admired most about him was his confidence. It wasn't cocky in the slightest, but it was fairly clear that he didn't let anything stop him from making a move, and I loved that. At one point, two guys were trying to chat me and my girlfriend up, and maybe he sensed that I wasn't into it, because he walked straight up to our group, interrupted whatever lackluster conversation was going on, and asked me to dance. I gave my friend the, "Sorry girl, you're on your own now" glance, and went off with my club bouncer in shining armor.

We went upstairs and started to display our talents at busting a move as everyone danced around us. He had rhythm, and I'm obviously a skilled dancer (not really, but I like to believe I am), so we were having a great time— and sure enough, that's when another girl attempted to kill the mood. "Let me show you some real dance moves," she told him while we were dancing together. Yeah, she tried it, and in all honesty, I wanted to throw hands while yelling, "You better step away from this man who's not my man but might very well be my man someday!" But I didn't, of course. I just waited to see what he was going to do about the situation, and he handled it beautifully. He put his hand up to create an invisible boundary between them, and simply stated, "I'm already dancing with someone," and completely dismissed her. Yep, I was smitten.

When our dance party came to an end, my feet were cursing me for my decision to wear the uncomfortable nude heels that I chose for the night. With what seemed like an endless amount of stairs to go down, I turned to him to prop my arm on his shoulder for some stability, but he had another idea in mind. He bent down, scooped me up over his bulging biceps and carried me honeymoon-style down the flight of stairs, carefully checking each step to make sure we wouldn't fall. I wanted to kiss him so badly, but I didn't. I just smiled at him, and he smiled back.

Because I was already enamored with this guy, I did what any woman would do—I looked him up online. I managed to find his Facebook, and it was then that I was greeted with a number of photos that made me uneasy. He was recently single from a long-term relationship, and the photos with his ex during their relationship were still there to see. She seemed perfect. My insecurities started to build and my wall was carefully being placed. I obviously didn't mention any of this to him at the time, but it made me move with caution, and he could sense it.

Once the weekend began to creep up, he asked if I was going to make my way down to the bars. Of course I wanted to see him, but none of my girlfriends were able to go out that night.

"Everyone's busy tonight, so I'm just hanging at home," I told him.

"Come alone and hang with me, then," he offered. Go out by myself? I'm independent, but even that was uncharted territory. Still, I decided to go for it. I slipped into one of my favorite red dresses, stepped into my rose gold heels, and off I went. Once I got to his bar, he came out to greet me with his usual big bear hug, and looked behind me to see if anyone was with me.

"Did you come alone?"

"I did."

"Nice, now you have to hang out with me."

He managed to sneak away from his duties for a bit to stroll down the street with me. We'd sit on a nearby bench and just talk about life. He asked if I would hang out and wait until he got off work, and of course I would. He walked me to my car at the end of the night, and I offered to drive him back to his. He was hesitant, out of embarrassment. "I drive a hoopty, so don't judge me," he explained. I just laughed and told him to get in.

We continued the small talk as I drove up to the roof where his car was parked, and once we pulled up to his spot, there was the anticipated linger that something was going to happen. We looked at each other for what seemed like an eternity, and he started to move in to kiss me. Instead of allowing myself to indulge in the kiss that

I'd been waiting weeks for, my gut had different plans, and I turned my head to give him my cheek. It shocked both of us, and the slight halt in his approach to plant the kiss on my face said more than his words ever would. He did ultimately kiss me on the cheek, and just smiled, but I saw the disappointment in his eyes. He thought I didn't like him, when in reality, I let my insecurities terrify me instead of just living in the moment.

We kept in touch, but it was different after that night. Plans always fell through and the effort on his end was fleeting. Feeling like it was all my fault, I tried to make up for what I did by overly expressing my desire for him and visiting him as much as possible, but it didn't seem to work. I constantly kicked myself for not just letting him kiss me, but I didn't want to be his rebound. I really liked this guy, and in an attempt to guard myself from getting hurt, I ended up hurting myself and someone else in the process.

Despite months of trying to build something, he ultimately chose to let whatever we had go, and cut communication with me. "I don't think we should talk anymore," he wrote me after expressing that perhaps my expectations for him were too high (read: I wanted some consistency, and I wasn't going to get it). Weeks later, I saw that he got back with his ex-girlfriend, and I was in a whirlwind of emotion that often comes with the unfortunate consequence of realizing someone you care about is no longer a part of your life.

There was nearly four months of no contact, until his birthday came around and I decided to send well wishes. That opened the line of communication again, and we'd tiptoe into that territory for years to come. During those months of no contact, he had graduated and moved back to his hometown up north, but once we made amends, we constantly checked in with each other, and even expressed our grievances in an effort to talk them out, even though we both knew nothing could really come of it. Still, there was a sense of comfort there that nobody else was able to provide me at the time.

I realized that when my apartment got broken into. I was in such a vulnerable and stressful state, and despite being hundreds of miles away, he made sure I was doing OK throughout the entire ordeal and what followed after the fact. He was able to be there for me more than others who could actually physically be there for me. That meant a lot. There was love there. There were unspoken feelings there. There was hope for a different ending, despite the circumstances, and as much as I tried to move on without him, it was very difficult. I compared every man to him, and I knew that wasn't fair, but in the back of my mind I always asked the same question, "If I'm here with another man, and he showed up at my door, would I stay here with this guy or leave with him?"

I would always leave with him.

Nearly two years after our first encounter, I finally expressed everything I felt for him, regardless of knowing he was in a relationship. I felt bad for it, and I knew it was selfish, but perhaps the distance provided me some sort of safety net. I told myself, "I'll speak my peace, since I know nothing could happen, anyway." So, that's exactly what I did. "I think about you often. I compare every man I meet to you. I was falling for you and it scared me. I didn't want to get hurt," I told him.

He called me to tell me how surprised he was, and to share that he thought of me often, too. He teased of inner demons, but wouldn't go into detail, just vague lines, like, "You don't want to get involved with someone like me." Why? I wanted to know why, but he offered me no explanations. Plus, what good would that do, anyway? He was in love with someone else, and our time had passed. I tried my best to let it go and move on. I wasn't going to insert myself into anything, especially out of respect for his relationship. If something was meant to happen between us, it would happen when the timing was right, but I couldn't keep pausing my life on the assumption of what could be, and miss out on what actually is. So, I started going on dates again. I was open to meeting people. I even started to gain actual feelings for other men, and then, it happened again.

Another two years after that conversation, while I was nursing a fresh heartbreak from another man who fell short of the potential that was presented to me, he reached out. We caught up like no time had passed, and he shared that his relationship had come to an end. We spoke as friends, healing each other, laughing with each other, opening up to one another. "No one cares about me the way you do," he confessed. That made me both happy and sad, but it hinted that perhaps there was something more here even after all this time, so I told him: "I'm actually visiting some friends in San Francisco next month. Would you want to meet up?"

"Absolutely."

We maintained contact leading up to the trip. His previous wishy-washy behavior had me a little cautious, but everything up until that point seemed promising. "Let me know when you land, and we'll find a place to meet up," he texted me the day before my flight. The giddiness of seeing the man who overwhelmed my mind and my heart for the past four years could not be contained. "Is this really happening?" I kept asking myself. Scenarios clouded my thoughts of what could happen once we reunited, what it would be like to see him again, what we'd talk about. I wondered if we'd finally have our first kiss. I couldn't wait to see what the weekend would unfold.

Once we touched down in Oakland, I sent him the anticipated, "We're here!" text. From getting our luggage, to waiting for our friend to pick us up from the airport, to unpacking and catching up, I had lost track of time, but when I checked my phone, there was still no response from him. Normally, that would send me down a spiral, but surprisingly, I didn't think much of it. "I'll hear from him," I told myself. My friends and I started to discuss the possible shenanigans we'd get into that night, and I relayed the message to him. "Hey, so we're thinking of going to these places tonight. Let me know if you'll be able to join us."

Nothing.

By the next day, having not heard from him, I quickly realized that he wasn't going to show. Once again, I was let down, and I couldn't even hide the pain anymore. Regardless of the span of years between our first interaction and our "breakup", if you could even call it that, it hit me like a ton of bricks. I was dealing with too much disappointment, both from him, from the man who had just broken my heart (you'll get that story, too, don't worry), and from myself. I was so angry at myself for believing that he would actually show up for me. I let out one big, hyperventilating cry on the bed, and my girlfriend, who had never seen me cry like that in all the years of our friendship, couldn't help but cry with me, too, and without any words, she simply just rubbed my back while we both stung from the pain of another let down.

When I returned home, I wrote him a message expressing my anger. I let him know that his behavior was unacceptable, and regardless of our past, "you don't treat a friend that way." This time he responded. "You're asking too much of me," he told me. That always seemed to be the case. I was always made to believe that I was asking for too much—too much time, too much attention, too much love, too much of anything because all I wanted was something, and I was never able to receive it. And so we were back to pretending to be strangers. We didn't talk anymore after that, and the animosity between us was thick.

But that's not the end of that tale.

Like clockwork, another two years passed before we spoke again. I remember thinking of him, and wondering if he was OK, and instead of letting the memory come and go, I figured enough time had gone by, so I acted on it. "Hey, thinking about you. I hope you're well," I texted him. No response. I accepted that this is how it would be. Our time was up, and I may not have complete closure on what really happened, but I got a crash course on the fact that closure was a luxury anyway, so I was (semi) OK with it. However, with life being the way it is, once I accepted what happened, I got a response.

"Hey! How have you been?"

Just like that, we were back into effortless conversation, but this one would remain embedded in my memory forever, because instead of dancing around the truth, we finally revealed ourselves to each other.

"I think there are things that need to be said," I started. "I was dealing with a lot of self-worth issues that I didn't even know I had. And so, when you turned me away, I felt rejected, and I acted out in response to that. I never felt good enough for you, but that was on me. I don't think you're a bad guy. I just had personal issues I was struggling with."

What he said next changed everything.

"Since we're being honest, there's something I need to tell you," he wrote. "You were never not good enough for me. The truth is, I was never good enough for you. For the last few years, I was battling a heroin addiction, and I had to push you away."

I was shocked. No one who knew him would have ever guessed that he was battling something like that behind closed doors, and for six years, I assumed all of his actions were a reflection of me. *He didn't love me. I wasn't good enough for him. I wasn't her, therefore, he didn't care about me.* When in reality, he did care. He cared so much that he chose to distance himself from me, because he knew the care I had for him would make me want to help him and try to fix him, which would only ultimately take me down with him. He pushed me away to protect me.

More importantly, it reminded me that not everything's about me. I would always take everything everyone did so personally, to the point where I would get physically sick about possibly saying the wrong thing and being at fault for situations not panning out the way I'd hoped, when the truth of the matter was, they're just dealing with things much bigger than me.

I cried for him. I cried at the thought of him having to keep this secret for so long, and at the thought of him having to deal with such difficult obstacles all on his own.

"Are you better now?" I asked him.

"I'm better in the sense that I don't do those things anymore," he explained, "But I feel so disconnected from everyone and everything now."

I expressed my gratitude for his bravery, and his willingness to share that with me, and reassured him that he'd always have a friend in me, should he ever feel the need to talk about it, but he didn't really want to talk about it.

We continued to check on each other here and there, and one day, he asked me a question that seemed to be straight out of my daydreams. "What are you doing this weekend?"

I'm sorry, what? Um... nothing?

He told me he'd be in town for work, and wanted to get together if I was willing to see him. Of course I was willing, but c'mon. We know his track record. This wasn't going to actually happen. Right?

Regardless, I said, "Sure!" and left it up to him to see it through without placing too much excitement on the idea that this would actually pan out. However, despite the doubt that lingered inside of me, when the night of our meet-up arrived, he actually followed through.

Nearly six years after being greeted with that smile, I was reunited with him again. I got dressed up, and we met at the same place where we first locked eyes on each other. The moment I saw him walking towards me, I felt as though I went into a time capsule and turned the dial back. He looked just as handsome as ever. He smiled the smile I remembered all too well and gave me a peck on the cheek to say hello.

"I can't believe this is actually happening," I told him.

"I know," he said.

"I didn't think you were actually going to come out," I admitted.

"I know, but I couldn't disappoint you again."

We sat down at Barney's Beanery, surrounded by drunk people acting, well, *drunk*, all around us, but our little table felt like an island far away from all of the commotion. We caught up over some cold glasses of beer, and then decided to stroll down the street like old times. During our walk, we came across his old place of work— the place where he took the photo of me and Lauren, the place where we had our first dance, the place where I knew I was going to fall deep for the stud with the dimples.

The owner recognized us, and told us to come inside for some shots on him. *Oh boy.* Suddenly, we were dancing on the same dance floor that I first became smitten with him, and I knew that if anything was going to happen, I was going to have to be the one to make the move. So I did. While dancing with each other, I turned to face him, I placed my hands on both sides of his face, and I pulled him in to finally have the kiss that was long overdue. Kissing him felt exactly as I'd imagined, but better, because it was real.

"Six years later," I told him.

"Worth the wait," he responded.

After a night of dancing and laughs, we decided to grab some junk food, because that's just how nights of drinking usually play out. While chomping on my chicken stars and ranch from Carl's Jr. in the car, the rain started to fall. "You're helping a lot of people, you know that, right," he said in regards to my writing. "Thank you," I told him. "Sometimes it's a little overwhelming, but I feel like I'm meant to do this."

As raindrops continued to pitter-patter on my windshield, he told me, "If I promise no funny business, can we continue this conversation at your apartment?"

"OK, but we're not having sex," I said.

"I just said we're not having sex," he laughed.

"I know, but I'm just confirming."

I was serious, too. Regardless of every rom-com I'd ever watched completely supporting the decision to have sex with him that night, I had been on an ongoing journey of abstaining from noncommittal sex for roughly over a year at that point, as an attempt to restructure my misguided perception of sex and dating (my journey was shared with the world in a personal essay published on Cosmopolitan). So, despite this being the perfect scene in every chick flick, I wasn't about to just throw all of that away.

We went back to my place, cuddled on the couch while watching *Friends*, and dozed off in each other's arms. I woke up to kisses from him, and had to question if it was reality or just another dream that I used to have often. But no, this was very real, and very, very surreal. We kept dozing in and out of sleep that morning until I had to drive him back to meet with his buddies that afternoon for his return up north. "I'll probably be coming out to LA more often," he reassured me. I smiled, and with a kiss, I said goodbye to him once more.

My girlfriends who were privy to his significance in my life were stunned at what happened.

"Was the spark still there? Are you guys gonna date now? How do you feel?" they'd ask me.

Sure, the idea of us pursuing something crossed my mind. After all, it was easy to remember why I initially fell for him, but during those six years, I grew. I evolved into a different woman, and despite always having care and love for him in my heart, that emotion shifted into something that wasn't the same as it was six years ago.

We briefly continued contact while he was away, but one day, a post I wrote called "Stop Thinking You're Hard to Love," prompted him to respond with his own thoughts on the matter, along with revealing some more truths for him. "The fact that you're a smart, strong woman doesn't intimidate me in the least bit, not worried about celibacy. It's the fact that any guy you talk to potentially becomes your writing material. And for a guy like me, who doesn't really share much of myself to people, it's too much," he wrote to me.

"If I could, I would just ask you to stop writing about that particular topic so we could date, but I just can't do that. I could never ask someone I care about to give up their passion. But I also realize if I truly care about you, I would do anything to help you, even if that meant for your future relationships."

This was a question often posed to me—"Aren't you worried that writing about this stuff will scare guys off?"

I could see that's where this was heading, so I told him what I tell everyone else.

"What I write *is* something I'm passionate about. I feel like I've found my purpose and that's not going to go away. It could shift, but again, it could not. I don't know. And I draw from my experiences, which means that, yes, you and other men of my past are a part of my story. I don't expect every guy to be cool with that, and just because you're not doesn't make you any less of a great guy. Just not the guy meant for me."

That was as honest as it could get. I knew the minute I began my journey writing and creating The Problem With Dating, it would affect my personal life, but that never really intimidated me. I felt very confident that what I was doing was part of what I was brought into this world to do, and that meant more to me than anything. I also knew that not everyone operates like me, so it was a given that some people would be turned off by my choice of career and decide to distance themselves from it. I could never be angry with that. I could never let that divert me from what felt right for me, either.

"You're right," he said. "The right guy will be cool with it. I wish you the best of luck."

When it came to sharing our story in this book, I was on the fence. I didn't want to disrespect his wishes in any way, because of the respect I have for him. However, I also know the value of our experience together, because of the lessons that were gained from it. So, while on the phone together a few months after our last conversation, I let him know that I'm writing a book, and he's part of it.

I could sense his hesitation, but ultimately, he gave me his blessing. I started to cry.

"What?! Why are you crying?"

"Because I never want to hurt you, and because I never want you to think your presence in my life was just for a story, because that's never the case."

"I know that," he reassured me.

And with that, one very long and open-ended chapter of my love life had finally come to a close, and I let every lingering "what if" go.

2

THE ONE I THOUGHT WAS "THE ONE"

THROUGH IT ALL I LEARNED THAT CLOSURE IS A LUXURY, NOT A GUARANTEE.

THIS SILENT EPIDEMIC BEING FOUGHT BEHIND CLOSED DOORS.

WE MAY FEEL AS THOUGH WE ARE DESERVING OF SOME FINAL BOW, BUT THE TRUTH IS NOBODY OWES US ANYTHING.

WE ARE GIVEN WHAT THOSE AROUND US DECIDE TO GRACE US WITH, AND SOMETIMES, ALL THEY CAN GIVE US IS THE CHOICE TO STOP STALLING OUR LIVES ON THE CLOCKS OF ANOTHER, AND FIND THE POWER WITHIN US TO TAKE THE FIRST STEP FORWARD ALONE.

It started like any modern-day fairy tale—with a swipe right. Yes, while the rest of the world was just finding a fling to hook up with for the night, I was trying to find someone I actually liked on Tinder. And believe it or not, it happened.

I had my fair share of interesting stories with guys I matched with on the dating app, but in all honesty, it was quite the feat to even get passed the messaging stage with me, because I pictured everything as if it were a scene coming out of Law & Order: SVU. If a guy came off the bat with a, "Hey, wanna grab drinks tonight?" I wouldn't even respond, because I felt like he was a serial killer. OK, if he was extremely hot, I'd respond, but definitely not agree to getting together. I know that may sound extreme, but this is a crazy world we live in.

Unlike Bumble, a similar dating app which differed in that it left it up to women to make the first move, I had the luxury of just sitting back and waiting to see which guy was interested enough to say something to me first. I know, women's privilege, and I used it to my advantage. But there was one guy in particular that I just couldn't wait any longer.

I still remember the moment he came up on my screen. I literally gasped. I was sitting at the dining table chatting about my day with my roommate while aimlessly swiping. Thank goodness I hadn't entered the left-swipe daze yet, otherwise I totally would've missed him completely. At what seemed like the perfect moment, I turned my eyes from our conversation down to my phone and I saw his face pop up. I threw my fingers back as an attempt to stop them from doing the usual swipe to the "no, thank you" bin and let out a huge, "OH MY GOD."

My roommate was obviously intrigued. "What?!"

"I just came across a guy on Tinder that I kinda semi-stalked a year ago on Instagram and I'm pretty sure we're meant to be together," I half-jokingly told her.

Here's the backstory: My Tinder Casanova and I had mutual friends. Well, mutual acquaintances, to be exact. They weren't people I could text and be like, "Hey, hook a sista up," but they were people who confirmed that he is:

1. Real.

2. Probably a decent person.

After looking through his photos to further prove his perfection, I gave him one hearty swipe right.

And whaddya know? MATCH. I swear I probably wet myself out of excitement just from the mere thought that he was interested in me, too. What was it about me that he liked? My wide variety of pics? My smile? My "I like short walks on the beach and peeing in the shower" bio?

I'd find out soon enough once he messaged me, I thought, because again, we're meant to be together...

Except he never messaged me.

Weeks and countless, meaningless conversations with guys I'd probably never remember (harsh, but true) went by, and I was ready to delete the app (ahem, again) to give myself a break from all of this digital so-called dating, but before I said goodbye to Tinder for what ended up being forever, I gave my matches another scroll to make sure I covcred all my bases before cutting the cord. And that's when I saw his profile again, just sitting there. My pride said, "Oh well, Bruna. If he liked you enough, he would've messaged you when he saw you matched." But everything else said, "Bruna, shut the fuck up and message this guy."

So I did.

After contemplating a bunch of witty intros, I ultimately decided that a simple "Hi" would do, because, "So you know we're gonna fall in love with each other, right?" seemed a little much. He messaged me back with a few curveballs to see if I could hang (he spoke to me in Spanish), and per usual, I knocked them out of the park (I used Google Translate). *I am a master communicator and clever as hell, sir. Do not try to test me.*

And that's when it started. Endless conversations from morning to night about absolutely everything and anything you could think of, from the darkest points of our lives to the fact that Seth Meyers' late-night set looked like a janitor's closet (which really is a bit unfair, he's a talented guy).

Of course, all of these memorable moments down memory lane were done through text, because who actually uses the phone anymore? Well, although that may be true, I needed to hear his voice, partially for insurance that this was legit and also because I'm old school when I'm actually interested in someone.

So after a few weeks of texting nonstop, I decided to give him a call without any warning. Ballsy, I know. To my surprise, his deep and alluring voice picked up, and we talked for an hour and a half while I lay in bed with the biggest smile on my face. We still hadn't met in person yet, which, given my prior statement about serial killers asking to hang out right away, would probably make you think that I was all about taking it slow, but here's the thing—I like taking it slow when I don't know if I like you yet. If I'm super into you, I tend to to put things into overdrive. I understand that's not my strongest quality, but that's how I looked at it, so dragging out this meeting started to irritate the shit out of me. Was I just a distraction? Was I just someone he intended to write all the time like a pen pal, but never actually pursue? My insecurities were eating all of this up, and adding a few failed attempts at getting together to the equation didn't help the situation.

However, during that phone conversation, he asked what I had planned for the weekend and offered to cook dinner for me. I almost passed out. Did he know the way to my heart is through my stomach? Either way, who is this man and how do I marry him?

A few days before our highly anticipated home-cooked first date, I brought up a very real, honest and vulnerable concern of mine that may have been a little too abrupt. I texted him, "Are you gonna flake on me again?"

Apparently, that was the wrong question to ask. He never responded. He didn't respond the next day or the day after that. On the day of our date, he didn't pick up my call, and it wasn't until the time he was already supposed to be at my apartment that he messaged me to say he wasn't coming, because he didn't appreciate what I said about him flaking. Instead of just chucking it in the fuck-it bin and moving on, I went into super apologetic mode, as I'd always do anytime something didn't work out.

I got nothing in return. For months, I got nothing from him, and as much as my ego would love to make it seem like it didn't matter because I hadn't even met the guy, I'd be lying. I was hurt as hell. That wasn't cool in my book.

It wasn't until late November of that year, two months after he decided to forget my existence and around the time I finally started to move on that he decided to pop back up in my life, because of course he did. I had been out celebrating my best friend's birthday, and for whatever reason, didn't feel sleepy enough to get in my PJs right away when I got home. So, I just posted up in bed to scroll through social media at 1 a.m. when a text bubble with his name popped up on my phone. I thought I was daydreaming again, all those nights wishing I'd see the dark bold letters spelling out his name light up on my phone, only to realize that probably wasn't going to happen again.

But this time it did.

He attempted to start small talk, asking about my Thanksgiving and telling me about his, but I couldn't play that game for very long. I told him what he did wasn't OK, and that I can't just act like nothing happened. He apologized and admitted his wrongdoing, explaining that he doesn't usually online date and it was all very surreal to him, because he didn't expect to hit it off so well with me. And then he asked if he could cook me dinner like he promised... in that moment.

"Well, it's 1:30 a.m., I don't have groceries and I'm not exactly hungry. But you can come over if you want."

"Are you sure?," he asked. "You're not gonna stab me with a knife?"

Interesting. Perhaps he was also an *SVU* fan?

"Mmm, no. I don't think so," I joked.

"OK, send me your address."

I understand my willingness to have this (technically) stranger come to my apartment in the middle of the night doesn't help with my serial killer argument, but I went for it, and look, I'm still alive.

I tried to remain cool, and not check my phone every five seconds in hopes of not putting too much anticipation into the matter, but let's be real—I was freaking out, and I was terrified he'd just cancel on me again. I checked my hair and makeup roughly 354 times before I got a text from him that read, "I'm downstairs."

Oh, shit.

He took the half-hour Uber ride from Mar Vista, Calif., to West Hollywood in the middle of the night, and I was about to throw up at the fact that we were finally going to see each other.

I went downstairs in my slippers (for the casual effect, of course) and there he was just on the other side of the glass door. I stood there and smiled, he smiled back, and I knew right there and then, he was either going to be my forever or he was going to ruin me. Whatever it was, I had never been more eager to find out.

I opened the door and gave him a big hug. The water bottle in his hand suggested that he might have been drinking that night, which made sense considering his surprising initiative. Perhaps the liquid courage helped shift all of this into motion. We walked through the garage to get to the elevator up to my apartment, and I couldn't even look him in the eye, I was so shy.

"Wait, let me look at you. I can't believe you're actually here," he told me. I must have instantly turned red because my insides were on fire.

My roommate was in Palm Springs for the weekend, so we had the place to ourselves. I gave him an over-exaggerated tour, since you could see the entire apartment in one swift glance from left to right. I showed him the living room space where I did my music meditation, and then I showed him my room, which he admired from the doorway, never stepping a foot inside.

I admired that about him. He never made me feel like I was just a sexual conquest, like so many men before him made me feel. He made it very clear that while he was attracted to me physically, he wanted to do this the "right way" (not letting sex overshadow everything), and I appreciated that so much. We sat down on the couch, facing each other and taking in our facial features and the fact that months of text bubbles had transformed into an actual human being. Our eyes never seemed to drift away from one another, as if we were in the presence of something we thought was just an elusive fairy tale, only to find out it's actually very real.

He apologized again for leaving without a trace, and I appreciated the verbal mea culpa. It's easy to say sorry through text. It's not as easy to say it face to face. He explained that he couldn't take the dating app seriously, and when we started talking, he didn't know what to make of it. He confessed that he didn't have a car at the moment and that he was living with his mom for the time being, and he felt ashamed by that, but I assured him that I didn't care about any of those things. He told me that he read everything I'd written to him multiple times and couldn't figure out how I was always able to say the perfect thing in the perfect way. He basically felt the same way I felt—that this, whatever *this* is, was too great to be real—but we handled it differently.

Instead of jumping in like me, he backed away out of fear and uncertainty. Not one to hold grudges, I forgave him and simply explained that I understood, but would appreciate that he communicate those feelings with me instead of going MIA.

There on the couch, when the rest of the world was sleeping, we dozed off into our own world, and in the midst of speaking about everything our hearts kept hidden, he leaned in and kissed me.

I felt like a young girl getting her first kiss. Time stopped and afterwards all I could wonder was if I did it right. Still, a smile couldn't help but escape my lips. We tried to watch a documentary together, but couldn't stop talking, so we shut off the TV and just let our thoughts flow freely while we held each other on the couch, stealing small kisses here and there.

Before we knew it, it was 6 a.m. "The sun is about to come up. Wanna see it with me," I asked, and he did. We walked out to the balcony to get a good view, and there it was. One of my favorite and most beautiful scenes with a guy who brought that same smile to my face. I took my phone out to take as many pictures as I could of the sunrise, attempting but constantly failing to capture its beauty, when I looked over and saw that he was taking pictures of me. I never saw those pictures, but the gesture made me giddy. After we walked back inside, I asked the only question that seemed to be left to ask. "Breakfast?"

We jumped in the car and went to one of my favorite 24-hour diners, Canter's, on Fairfax. We slid into the booth and snuck glances at our menus when we were able to peel our eyes off of each other. "You have a beautiful smile," he told me. I smiled even bigger. While inhaling our coffee and scrambled eggs, we dove back into conversation about our childhoods and family. At one point we discovered our mutual admiration for the Gypsy Kings, thanks to our mothers blasting Spanish music when we were young. We even started to sing "Bamboleo" out loud together, humming over the same line in the song that neither of us knew the lyrics to, and jumping back in together on "vivir asi!" It's a moment I'll never forget.

"When we first started talking, you mentioned that you're only having fun," I began to say to him.

"That's not what this is," he reassured me. *Phew.*

When it came time to pay the check, I saw him reach for his wallet. Little did he know, he had left it in my living room.

I saw it there on the coffee table before I closed the door, but I didn't say anything to him, because I knew he'd never let me pay for breakfast, and I don't know, I guess I wanted to repay him for the best morning of my life. So I kept quiet and just silently enjoyed the terror on his face.

"Oh, my, God. I left my wallet at your house! I can't believe I did that. How could I have done that, I'm so embarrassed."

I laughed, and in my usual sarcastic tone, told him, "Wow, I'm not sure I can afford this $13 bill."

I knew it had nothing to do with the actual price of the check, and later on, I told him the truth.

He wasn't pleased, but there was a part of him that felt charmed by the whole thing. The other funny part about the whole wallet-left-behind scenario is that during our breakfast outing, my roommate came back home, and upon finding a random wallet in the living room, opened it up to see whose it was. She instantly text me his name in all caps with a bunch of "?!?!?!"

"I have a lot to tell you," I discreetly texted her back.

We returned to my apartment around 9 a.m., and after an impromptu yet amazing and unforgettable 7 hours together, it was time to bid adieu. He grabbed his wallet, gave me a hug and kiss at the door, and we said our goodbyes. I tried to sleep, because I knew I had to. I'd been awake for about 24 hours at that point, but the natural high of what happened wouldn't let me. A few hours later, while Christmas shopping with my best friend, he texted me, and we picked up right where we left off.

The daily conversations continued, and the pep in my step each day was undeniable. I felt like I was living a fairy tale. I felt validated. I felt like the guy I always knew I wanted and the love I always felt I deserved was finally here. It was real. It was amazing. It was mine.

"Can I take you out on a real date?" he asked me.

He made us reservations at this Italian restaurant by the beach and I was so fucking nervous. I went to the mall earlier in the day to buy a completely new outfit (because obviously nothing I already owned was good enough) and he knew this so he made fun of me. "Did you find a prom dress for tonight yet," he texted me. "Also, I hope you don't mind that my parents come. Figured we can just knock it all out at once," he joked. He made me laugh. Ugh, I liked him so much.

When I finally got to the restaurant that night, he greeted me with a kiss on my cheek, and I think he tried to pull my chair out for me but I totally didn't even catch that (because, unfortunately, I've become blind to chivalry) so I just went to the other chair and sat down. It wasn't until he made a subtle facial reaction that I realized what had happened.

The moment we sat at the table, the conversation and connection sparked, per usual. It took us almost 15 minutes to even order our food because we didn't care about the menu, we were too focused on each other. We held hands at the table, he complimented how I looked, he asked all the right questions and he even gave me a gift. Yes, he gave me a damn gift! "I brought you something," he said to me, and handed me a mix CD of his favorite music. I can't even begin to explain how much I loved that he did that. Flowers are cool, chocolate is obviously welcome, but to take the time to make something that actually has meaning is something I value very much. "It's a mix of all my favorite songs," he told me, and when I heard it later that night, I knew it was more than just his favorite music. He always said, "Music is what feelings sound like," and on that CD, he was giving me a glimpse into his heart the best way he knew how. He wasn't a writer like I was, and his previous actions suggested that open communication about what's going on with him wasn't the easiest, so when it came to expressing himself, the songs spoke for him, and it was beautiful.

We drank wine. We ate off each other's plates, we laughed a lot and we asked the types of questions we really wanted to know the answers to. When it was time for dessert, he read my mind (or my facial expressions) when the tray of options was presented to us and figured out that I wanted tiramisu. We shared it and split the last piece.

When dinner was done, a part of me was sad. I didn't want to seem selfish, but I didn't want the night to end. Luckily, it didn't. Despite not mentioning any other plans beforehand, he looked at me after paying the bill and asked if I'd ever been to the Venice Canals. I told him no, but that I'd always wanted to go. We ended up getting in the car, putting on his mix, and off we went.

The canals were absolutely breathtaking. Each bridge was lit up for the holiday season, causing a twinkle in the water that looked straight out of a magazine. At one point, I ended up standing underneath the mistletoe without even knowing it, and he stepped in, pulled me close and kissed me. It was perfect. We continued to stroll, taking in all of the multi-million dollar homes that inhabit it and playing make-believe on living in one of the mansions. Then, he asked me to "come here" so we could take a picture together. I snuggled up to him with the canals behind us, and he snapped a photo of us. His selfie skills weren't on par with mine (granted the lighting was not the greatest) so it's a fuzzy, poorly lit photo, and I loved it so much.

At one point, he mentioned that the beach was walking distance from the canals, to which I slyly alerted him that I always have a beach towel in my trunk for impromptu trips. It became clear that this night wasn't going to end any time soon.

We grabbed the towel from the car and he took me on this tiny excursion to the beach. We kicked off our shoes and enjoyed the sand, then ran to the water to dip our toes in the ocean. If this is sounding like a scene straight out of a movie, that's because it practically was. After frolicking in the freezing and kind of terrifying dark ocean, we went back to the sand and sat down. He curled himself behind me, throwing his jacket on me to keep me warm, and held me as we listened to the waves and some music on his phone while talking about family, the future, our fears, our dreams—you name it. The things he asked me made me feel like this was far from a fling. He wanted to see if something substantial with us was possible, and so far, nothing proved otherwise.

As our late-night beachy rendezvous came to a close, he asked me another question: "Wanna go to the movies?" After all this, he still wanted to spend time with me. I couldn't explain the joy I was feeling, but as you may have assumed, I said hell yes, and we grabbed our shoes and began our journey to the next destination.

Once we got back in the car, we continued listening to his CD while making our way to the theater to catch a late showing of *Birdman*. Now, it's clear my emotions and my mind are on cloud 9, but there was one thing that kept trying to kill the moment. My period. I unfortunately got a visit from Aunt Rose shortly before the date started, so as much as I wanted to just surrender to this magical date, I was also slightly panicking about leaving a mark everywhere we sat. Luckily, that didn't happen, but when we got to the theater, I bee-lined it to the bathroom to make sure that I was A-OK, and spoiler alert! I was not. I leaked through everything. The SVU analogy finally caught up with me and there was a crime scene happening in my pants. I was freaking out.

Of course, the stall I was in had no toilet paper, because clearly this rom-com was teetering too much on the rom side and needed some com to balance out.

There was no one else in the bathroom, so I had to MacGyver it up until one mystery woman walked in and I cried for help. I was so happy to see that hand under my stall with a wad of fresh TP. I did what I could with the situation, knowing that I was already in the bathroom for a significant amount of time and needed to get back out there.

Once I walked out, he gave me a face that suggested he thought I had the shits. That was terrifying, so I came up with the best lie I could. "Sorry! Of course my stall had no toilet paper and my zipper got stuck, so I had to deal with that." He probably didn't believe me, but he laughed it off, and told me that he bought us some Sour Patch Kids to snack on (he kindly gave me all of the red ones because they're my favorite, and I learned that he liked the yellow ones, which is really great, because it's nice to know someone likes the yellow ones). We watched the movie while being all curled up with each other, my head on his shoulder and our hands clasped together. Afterwards, I drove him home, he kissed me goodnight in the car, and I drove off with the feeling of love completely consuming me from what I had experienced the last seven hours.

The next day, he texted me to tell me that he couldn't stop thinking about me, something every girl loves to hear from the guy she's obsessed with. Being the curious girl I am, I decided to pry.

"Oh, really? What were you thinking about?" And that's when he sent me something I would read over and over and over again for years.

DEAR BRUNA,

I LOVED SITTING THERE, ON THE SAND, HOLDING YOU. WALKING THE CANALS, CROSSING BRIDGES WHEN WE GOT TO THEM LOL. YOU HAVE SUCH A WARM HEART. NO MATTER WHAT CRAP YOU'VE DEALT WITH IN THE PAST WITH YOUR EXES, YOU STILL MAINTAIN SUCH A HUMBLE AND BEAUTIFUL OUTLOOK ON LIFE. I FELT LIKE YOU WERE TELLING ME MY STORY MUCH OF THE TIME AT DINNER. I LIKED SEEING THE SMILE ON YOUR

FACE WHEN WE BOTH DECIDED ON TIRAMISU, AND THE
SIDE EYE YOU GAVE ME WHEN WE SAW THE RED
VELVET. I LOVED HOW OPEN YOU WERE TO JUST
TAKING YOUR SHOES OFF AND RUNNING INTO THE
WATER WITHOUT WORRYING ABOUT A THING. YOU
REMINDED ME TO APPRECIATE THE SMALL AND SIMPLE
THINGS THAT MONEY CAN'T BUY. I LOVED YOU
RESTING YOUR HEAD ON MY SHOULDER WITH YOUR
ARM AND FINGERS ALL WRAPPED UP WITH MINE. I
MUST SAY, I LIKE GETTING TO KNOW YOU BRUNA. THE
END FOR NOW.

I was falling in love with this man, and I didn't care how little or how long we knew each other. He made me feel like magic. He supported my dreams and always offered to help make whatever ideas I came up with a reality. He got on the guitar to learn Blackbird by the Beatles after finding out it was my favorite song. He offered to give me his MacBook when I said I needed a new computer to build my business. He was everything I knew I wanted, but was too afraid didn't exist. And yet, here he was. Not a figment of my imagination or a composite of a man I was told to love through romantic comedies. A real man, who exceeded whatever expectation I could possibly have, and he felt the same way about me.

That week after our date we kept in constant communication, and on that Friday, we tried to figure out a time during the weekend that we could see each other. He laid out his itinerary, as did I, and we both realized it was going to be a tough squeeze. "Well, I don't care if it's just for a little, I just want to see you," I offered. "Of course, love," he answered. We moved on to different water cooler conversations after that, but I noticed he wasn't responding. "He's with his friend, he'll respond later," I told myself.

Except he didn't. He didn't respond later that night. Or the next day. Or the day after that.

Suddenly, I felt the heaviness in my chest as I was entering into familiar yet unwelcome territory. *There's no way he'd ghost me after all of that*, I thought. Something must be wrong. I called, but no answer. I left a message, but no call back. I stalked social media to make sure he was OK, but there was nothing being posted. Just when I was about to entertain the idea of calling the SWAT team to make sure he wasn't lying in a ditch somewhere, I saw that he liked a girl's photo on Instagram (that Following tab is *dangerous*). OK, so he's still alive and liking other girls' pictures and just ignoring me. Cool. I was a livid.

A few weeks went by with no word from him, and because timing is always so perfect, I had finally received the gift I got him for Christmas. A handcrafted piece of wall art that read, "You're making me dance inside," an ode to his favorite singer, Sade, and a nod to the fact that he makes music and I love to dance. I got it framed. I wrapped it. I printed our selfie from our date, put it in a very thoughtful card I wrote for him, and I went to deliver it to him. I asked Lauren to accompany me for moral support, and although she wasn't sure this was the best idea, she knew I had to do it (notice a trend?). His address was still in my GPS history, so I pressed go, and off we went. I left it in a common area, hoping no one would steal it, and took a picture, which I sent to him with a message saying, "I got this for you before everything happened, and I still want you to have it. Merry Christmas."

I finally felt free again. Something about just leaving the gift there felt like it was my gateway to just moving on, even if I didn't have closure. And, yet again, that's when he decided to say something. While checking my email the next morning, a few days before Christmas, I saw the following:

HI BRUNA. I'M GOING TO KEEP THIS EMAIL SHORT AND TO THE POINT. FIRST, I WANT TO APOLOGIZE FOR BEING NON EXISTENT RECENTLY. IT'S A PRETTY EASY EXPLANATION, I'M SIMPLY NOT READY TO JUMP BACK INTO THE DATING/RELATIONSHIP SCENE. I'VE DONE A LOT OF THINKING, AND IT'S JUST NOT IN ME RIGHT NOW AND I AM NOT GOING TO WASTE ANYMORE OF YOUR TIME. I NEED TO GET RIGHT WITH MYSELF AND MY LIFE BEFORE I CAN SHARE IT WITH SOMEONE ELSE. I WANT YOU TO KNOW THAT YOU ARE A WONDERFUL PERSON, BRUNA. I HAD A GREAT TIME WITH YOU AND GETTING TO KNOW YOU, NO REGRETS ON MY END. ALSO, I RECEIVED YOUR GIFT AND YOUR CARD THIS MORNING AND I DON'T REALLY KNOW WHAT TO SAY. TOTALLY UNEXPECTED. THAT WAS VERY SWEET AND THOUGHTFUL OF YOU THOUGH, THANK YOU SO MUCH.

WITH THAT SAID, I WANT TO WISH YOU THE BEST IN EVERYTHING THAT YOU DO. I KNOW YOU DON'T NEED

ME TO REMIND YOU, BUT YOU ARE GOING TO DO
SOMETHING VERY SPECIAL IN THIS WORLD, BRUNA.
TAKE CARE OF YOURSELF.

It took me a moment to realize what just happened, and when I did, I fell back into my dark hole. I should have just left it at that. I should have let it go. I should have taken the L and moved forward, picking up whatever pieces I could, but I didn't. I wrote back an incredibly long email, pleading for him not to do this, not to let me go, not to make me pick up the pieces, but in his usual demeanor, I was left with nothing but silence.

I wish I could say that was the end of it to save face, but I'd be lying. For months I became handicapped by the thought of him. I'd drink bottles of wine to myself and write to him just to get nothing back. At one point, I almost felt like there wasn't a human on the other end of that phone anymore, so my dignity didn't care to weigh in on whether or not I should leave the poems and letters unsent. I would drown in memories of him, constantly scrolling through his photos and keeping an eye on his social media just to feel some sort of connection to what he was doing. My friend called me an emotional cutter. "You know you only get hurt when you look, so why do you look?"

"It's all I have left," I told her.

I felt pathetic, and that shame stuck around for a long time. The desperation was so palpable, and it only got worse. Almost six months after receiving the email of doom, I found out a friend from high school had passed away, and death always tends to put things into perspective.

Instead of the "why did you leave, come back" feelings I felt, I was feeling angry and my fingers jumpstarted a fiery text that I sometimes wish I could take back. I went off on him, telling him that life is too short to hold out for a guy who doesn't even have the decency to tell me what the fuck happened, that I deserve better than that, that I'm sorry I made him feel something real and he was too scared to do anything about it. After I sent that, I saw the bubbles start forming on his end and I nearly passed out. That's when I remembered there actually is another person at the other end of this thing, and he wasn't exactly welcoming to my lash-out.

He told me I took it too far and that I'm beginning to sound like a "stalker." He asked me to delete his number and never speak to him again. He blocked me on social media, and just like that, I became "the crazy girl." I wasn't happy about it then, and I'm definitely not happy about it now, but all I could do at that point was try to learn from my mistakes.

Media and society place so much importance on needing closure from another person in order to move on, but the truth is that closure is a luxury, and we don't always get it. Even when I pushed his buttons to get a rise out of him in hopes of getting closure, it just blew back up in my face. I took a trip to Spain to try and escape everything that happened, but he was still there with me. I heard a violinist playing one of the songs he put on the CD he gave me while walking down the street in Madrid. I heard a group of men playing Gypsy Kings' "Bamboleo" in the middle of a small town in Granada. I saw him with every sunrise and sunset for the next two years. In such a short time, I gave this man so much power over me, and he was haunting every moment of my life, because I allowed him to.

With time, I slowly but surely started to regain myself without his memory hovering over it. I no longer dreamed of what could've been and embraced what was. I decided I couldn't waste any more moments of my life thinking about someone who so willfully chose not to be a part of it. Even then, I must admit, there were plenty of times when I wondered what would happen if he came back, because they almost always do. I wondered if I'd give him another chance. I'd see his friends out and about and my heart would stop at the thought of seeing him, but I never did. And although many guys from my past would resurface, he was not one of them.

I began to do a lot of things to focus on bettering myself emotionally, mentally and spiritually, because this experience forced me to face a lot of undesirable qualities about myself. Why did I fall for guys so easily and so fast? Why did I place all of my validation in someone else's hands? Why would I cripple the second they walked away? Why was this always happening to me?

I started doing yoga consistently, I was meditating, I was writing a lot. I was meeting new people, I was open to new bonds, and I was always fully aware of what was happening in my life. I was accepting what the Universe was telling me and encouraging it to continue giving me signs because I was paying attention. And this began my self-love journey.

One night, I did a full moon ritual and wrote down my intentions. One of the things I wrote down was to let go of hope for a relationship that wasn't meant for me. The next day, for the first time in two years, I saw a photo of him kissing a girl, and got the sign I needed to move on. He was in a relationship with someone and that someone wasn't me, and it was never going to be me because he wasn't meant for me. I had to learn to accept that and I had to learn to let go.

And by the power of persistence, grace and whatever higher power has been guiding me, I did, along with the desire of trying to know why he chose to let me go.

3

THE ONE I TRIED TO FIX

I STOOD IN FRONT OF HIM WITH TEARS IN HIS EYES.

HE ASKED IF I STILL LOVED HIM, AND I COULDN'T LIE.

TIME TOOK A TOLL ON US, WE DRIFTED APART.

HE REFUSED TO SEE IT HAPPEN, BUT I KNEW IN MY
HEART.

THIS WAS NOT A FOREVER THING.

THIS WAS JUST RIGHT NOW.

THREE YEARS OF LOVE CAME TO AN END WITHOUT
REALIZING HOW.

I'M SORRY, I SAID. I HAVE TO LEAVE.

HE'D TRY TO PULL ME CLOSER, TUGGING AT MY
SLEEVE.

HE LOVED ME. THIS MUCH I KNOW.

BUT WITH HIM I'D NEVER GROW.

THE ONLY MAN TO THIS DAY, WHO OPENLY ADORED
ME.

AND I BROKE HIS HEART SO THAT I COULD BE FREE.

The One I Tried to Fix

As you can tell by now, I had my fair share of *almost-but-not-quite* relationships (or situationships, as I like to call them) with guys once I was single and back on the market. My last actual boyfriend was probably the closest thing I had to experiencing that sweet, innocent (and committed) love you hear about in the movies, but it was still riddled with problems.

One of my favorite things about working at Starbucks during college was the ability to meet so many different people every single day. Whether it was a rich businessman, a thirsty homeless person, a mom wrangling her kids, a couple on their first date, a truck driver getting ready for his graveyard shift or just your regular Joe Schmoe, I quickly realized that people from all walks of life loved to make a quick stop at Starbucks.

Including my future ex-boyfriend.

When he first came in with his buddies, I was captivated by his smile (of course). However that admiration was instantly followed by shame, because his baby face made me believe that my thoughts were on the verge of cradle robbing. So, I let it go, but I'd be lying if I said I didn't flush with excitement whenever he came in. At one point, I confessed my infatuation to my coworker, who, to my delight, revealed that my coffee crush was actually my age.

"Oh, we went to high school together! He graduated our year," he told me. Oh, thank goodness! But now what? Sure, your average female may not do a thing and let the men flock to her, but that's not how I operated. When I saw something I wanted, I did everything I needed to do to get it. Or at least try. This quality was great when it came to work, but in love, it wasn't the best attribute.

My best approach at the time, so as not to come off too creepy and forward, was a MySpace friend request. He was a regular, so he knew of me and MySpace was all the rage at that time, so I figured that wouldn't be weird. I was greeted with a message back from him instantly that read, "Hey, it's my favorite Starbucks barista!"

Oh, if he only knew what was to come.

His visits had a different feeling in the air after that, like two teenagers who tried to keep their crush for each other under wraps even though it was totally obvious. I would get that giddy nervous feeling whenever he came in, and he and his friends would simmer down to a whisper whenever I went outside on my breaks. They were talking about me. *Good*, I thought.

One day, I had gone across the street to get my usual orange chicken and chow mein Panda Bowl for lunch, which I never seemed to be able to finish. Since I had leftovers, I walked outside to greet him and his friends and held out the food, "Are you hungry?"

"Yeah, thanks," he responded.

Now, normally I would leave this minor detail in the memory bank and not feel as inclined to share, except I later learned that moment was a defining factor for him. Years later, I asked him when he realized that he really liked me, and he told me, "When you offered me your food, I thought that was really sweet." Ladies, food really is a way to a man's heart.

But I digress...

After feeding him, I gave him my number, and anxiously checked my phone every few minutes the rest of the night expecting *something*, *anything* from him. But my phone screen was blank. That was not OK with me, so, shortly before closing, I noticed one of his friends walk in alone, and I took matters into my own hands.

"Hey, what can I get you?"

"Venti iced coffee, please," he told me, and that's when I made my move.

"You're friends with *[ha, I'm not telling you his name]*, right?"

"He's my brother, actually!"

"Oh, nice! Well, how about this? I'll give you your Venti iced coffee for free if you give me his number."

I think he was both surprised and entertained with how forward I was, but he happily obliged, and I gave him his beverage on the house in exchange for his brother's digits. I went to my phone and texted him.

"You took way too long to text me," I wrote.

"I thought I'm supposed to wait three days?" he responded.

"If you would've waited three days, you would've lost me already."

God, I was so aggressive. It's clear to see my masculine energy was alive and thriving. At that point, he got a sense of the type of woman he was dealing with, and didn't waste any more time. He asked me out on a date, and, of course, I said yes. But do you think I waited until our date to see him again? Absolutely not. We ended up seeing each other the night before our planned outing on a whim. We met up and just hung out in the car and talked into the night. At one point, even though we both knew our actual date was happening the next night, we decided to skip a few steps and have our first kiss right there. It was so innocent and sweet. I felt like a girl straight out of an ABC Family movie. The second I got out of his car and left, I couldn't wait to see him again.

The next night, he picked me up and we went to have sushi for our date. He taught me how to properly fold my chopstick wrapper so that it could serve as a stand for my chopsticks while I ate, and we dove into great conversation over some spicy tuna and shrimp tempura. Afterwards, he asked if I wanted to go to his house and meet his friends. Some may feel like that's a bit soon and super random, and you're not wrong, but I was already into him, so I thought—why not?

I went over to his house with him, played some basketball outside and then met his brothers and friends (some of whom were familiar Starbucks faces). I felt so comfortable with all of them, and they were so welcoming with me, which only fueled that giddy *this-is-totally-gonna-be-a-thing* feeling. Except...oh, that's right. I was also dating someone else.

Once I realized that something was brewing here, I openly explained to him that I was also talking to someone else. He was receptive but quickly let me know, "I don't like to share." So, I had a decision to make, and in all honesty, it was an easy one. I called up the other guy and told him that I'd met someone else, and I wanted to explore that relationship. He said he understood, and before I knew it. I was snowballing into a relationship.

Everything happened so fast.

About a week after our first date, I met his mom, then I met his extended family at his birthday dinner, and then, roughly one month later, he asked me to be his girlfriend through a written note hidden in Jell-O (I love me some strawberry Jell-O). Throughout that time, I got to know more of his friends and quickly realized that his house was known as the party house, because it was rarely ever empty. Weekends were for kickbacks and house parties, and that's when the red flags that I subsequently ignored for a long time began to spring up.

I didn't want to see any problems with us, because I finally had the type of relationship that I heard about. I was finally attracted (mentally, physically and emotionally) to a good guy who saw the value in me and didn't hesitate to act on it. He was romantic and thoughtful. He made me dinner after a long day. He brought flowers for my mother when they met and made an effort to befriend my friends. He would leave me love notes on my car while I was at work and never let a moment pass by without completely professing his love to me.

But there were problems, and no matter how perfect we looked in pictures, or how much love fueled by good intention there was in our relationship, neither one of us could hide from the fact that our issues were bigger than the both of us.

And it all hit me at once.

The routine of ignoring the seriousness of his drinking started to become an old habit I was desperate to kick, but didn't have the courage to quit. I gave him another ultimatum, and maybe he knew I was bluffing, but his answer still stung like a shot through the heart.

"If you drink tonight, I'm leaving," I said with as much strength as I could muster up.

"OK," he told me. "Let me grab your stuff."

I didn't see it then, but it became clear as day after the fact. The relationship I put on a pedestal was barely off the ground, and he may have loved me as deeply as he knew how, but that just wasn't enough to keep us afloat.

I was never much of a party animal or a drinker, so I always thought I was just being naïve about what I was experiencing with him. He, on the other hand, was the MVP. He never declined a drink, and it didn't take him long before he was sloppily walking around his own house party slurring about *who-knows-what* while slinging an arm over someone's shoulders and using their body as support to stand up.

He's just having fun. This is what people our age do. Right?

Except I began noticing the hold alcohol had on him, and I was quickly thrown into a situation I wasn't sure I could handle.

I was worried, but again, I thought I was the exception to the rule, because it felt like I was the only girl who wouldn't get wasted every possible chance she got. His friends weren't worried, so maybe I was overreacting. I turned a blind eye and masked my frustration with excuses.

Plus, I loved him, and for the first time in my life, I knew he loved me back. He thought about us. He planned a future for us. He never shied away from making me feel important to him, and those were feelings I wasn't ready to give up at the time.

I just didn't know that I'd have to share that priority in his life with the bottle.

The blackouts were a common occurrence. I'd wake up the next morning to him looking over at me and asking, "Babe, what happened?" *What happened was I was up all night making sure you didn't act like a damn fool and cleaned up after all of your drunk friends. That's what happened.*

At one point it just became too much, and I stopped bluffing.

I spent two years watching over my boyfriend like I was his mother, constantly crying and fighting over his need to drink and not being able to understand the importance of it all.

I tried everything. I stopped drinking for a year and a half so he wouldn't feel obligated to throw one back like everyone else—*See, babe, you're not alone. I'll be sober with you*—but that didn't work. Nothing worked. Because what I refused to acknowledge during that whole time was the simple fact that you can't help people who don't care to help themselves.

So, one day I decided I was done and I left. I walked away from a man who wanted to marry me, a man who, in the public eye, seemed great for me, but I knew that the reality of the matter behind the facade everyone else saw was a downward spiral. And even after knowing that, I still felt guilty for leaving because I thought I abandoned someone I cared about.

Then one night before heading out to a party in an effort to distract my emotions, I got a disturbing call from him. I watched his name flash on my screen for a few rings before deciding to answer.

"I crashed my car!" he yelled. I asked what happened, but he couldn't explain. Shock? Maybe. Drunk? Yes. Despite denying that he was driving under the influence, I heard it in his voice. I knew that tone. I hated that tone.

He drove drunk and lost control of the steering wheel on the on-ramp of the 210 eastbound freeway, flipping his car 50 feet and landing in the carpool lane facing the opposite way of traffic. Of course, I didn't know all of this at the time.

Anticipating a fender bender (yet still frantic), I got in my car to go find him on the freeway. I kept trying to call him to figure out what was going on, but at one point, a California Highway Patrol officer told me to stop calling because it was an open investigation, and turned off his phone.

That's when I realized this was much more serious than I could imagine. Once I was near the area of the accident, I kept looking on the shoulder to see if I could find him and a cop pulled over. What I saw instead was a sea of flashing red lights–multiple fire engines, police cars, and ambulances shutting the entire highway down on the opposite side of the freeway. It felt like a bad dream.

How will I get to him?

I'll tell you this—you start coming up with some crazy solutions when there are obstacles stopping you from reaching someone you love. I contemplated getting on the next on-ramp and reversing all the way down the freeway to where the scene of the accident was. But, I didn't. I needed to be rational.

I couldn't get to him, that was the harsh truth I had to accept, and I'd never felt so helpless in my life. By the time traffic moved to the point of the accident, he was long gone, along with his totaled car.

I was able to find out which hospital he was taken to, so I called his brother to let him know what happened since I was the only call my ex made and no one knew what was going on. His family, who was angry with me for breaking his heart, showed up and found me crying in the waiting room.

The hospital wouldn't let me see him while he was handcuffed to the hospital bed. Even his own mother was given about a minute with him, and she told me she'd let him know I was there. I needed him to know I was there.

I spent that night in his bed, waking up every hour thinking he was going to come in and lie down next to me, and then I remembered–*He's not coming, Bruna. He's in jail.*

The next morning I called the holding cell every hour until they could tell me what time he was going to be released. When I finally got an answer, I went with his mother to pick him up, and was amazed to see that he was able to get away from that accident with nothing but scratches on his arms.

I was so angry. I was so sad. I was so grateful he was still alive. "I know you knew this would happen to me," he told me. My heart sank because it was true. "Doesn't mean I wanted it to," I replied.

As mad as I was, I couldn't leave him alone now. So I stayed by his side, trying to get his life back on track. I drove him to school, work, his counseling meetings and even went to AA with him to prove that he didn't have to fight this addiction alone.

But again, it wasn't enough. Nothing was enough.

Even after everything that happened—nearly killing others and himself because he was being reckless and made a poor decision—he still didn't think he had a problem. "I'm only going to these things because the court is making me," he would tell me, and I couldn't even come up with words to respond, because I knew he wasn't trying to hear me.

During that time, I realized he was drinking behind my back. We'd continue to have blow-up fights over his addiction and I grew resentful of him and the entire situation. I felt like I put my life on hold for someone who was ungrateful. I know my involvement was a choice, but it didn't feel that way at the time, and no matter what I did, it seemed to be for nothing.

That resentment led me to doing something I didn't share with anyone for years, something I pushed so far back into my mind that I'd have to question if it even happened, because my shame of the matter was too great to acknowledge it.

I cheated.

It was so outside of my character, and it burned a hole through me. Still, I never told him. I just buried it deep inside and tried to act like it never happened, but of course it did, and my conscience would never let me forget it. I was a coward, and I let my cowardice justify doing something that was against everything I believed in.

On the anniversary of his accident, I called it quits. I didn't plan for it to happen that way, but I guess subconsciously, I realized that another year went by, and instead of seeing the progress I'd hoped for, we regressed, both individually and together. He continued drinking, but just chose not to tell me, and I began putting my integrity in question. That wasn't a position I wanted to be in.

It hurt to say goodbye, because he was someone I cared for and it felt like I was giving up, but I didn't like the person I was becoming in that relationship.

A few months after our breakup, I ran into him at the local bar. He was drunk, which was no surprise to me, and proceeded to follow me out when I tried to leave. He grabbed my keys and yelled, "You're too drunk to drive," but I wasn't. I had one beer. He, on the other hand, was too drunk to do anything, and he used that moment to express what I could only assume he had been holding in for some time.

"I was never good enough for you!" he yelled at me in the middle of the parking lot. "No matter what I did, I was never good enough for you. You never loved me!"

I was so angry with him and taken aback that he could even question my love when I devoted so many years to him, but, maybe he was right. Was I really in it for him? Or was this another "project" I refused to give up on? I definitely cared for him, there's no denying that, but my unfortunate actions always made me wonder about my actual commitment to the relationship. Did I cheat because I was fed up or did I cheat because I just didn't care anymore? Did I cheat because I wanted payback for the pain he caused or because I wanted a way out of the relationship I was too afraid to let go of?

I wish I had the answers to all of those questions, but the only conclusion I can come up with is the fact that I held on to something for the wrong reasons.

I should have left for good the night he made it so painfully clear that the bottle was more important to him than I was, but I was too blinded by the potential of a relationship that wasn't as harmful and unhealthy as the ones from my past. And that desire to experience something "normal" served as a great mask to the fact that I was trying to make what we had seem better than it was.

I just wanted him to love me, and I believe a part of him really did, but the truth is I stuck it out for my own gain. Of course, I wanted to see him well and healthy, but I also saw an opportunity to fix something, and I thought by fixing it, there would be value in my love. I thought by fixing him, my love would be healing and deserving.

I was mistaken.

There was never enough room in his heart for me, because whether he was willing to accept it or not, the liquor filled him up more than I ever could.

The only one who needed my fixing was me. The only one who needed my healing was me. But that was a harsh truth that I wasn't willing to accept for a very long time.

And with that, I let my misdirected healing and desire for control go.

4

THE ONE WHO CHALLENGED ME

MY FEAR WAS THAT I WAS NEVER ENOUGH.

WHAT IF I WAS SOMEBODY NOBODY CAN LOVE?

INSECURITIES ARE LOUD, NO MATTER HOW HARD I'D
TRY TO SILENCE THEM.

THE VOICES IN MY HEAD REALLY MADE ME BELIEVE.

"SILLY GIRL. HOW COULD YOU EVER COMPETE?"

'YOU'RE RIGHT,' I THOUGHT.

'WHO'D WANT ME?

A LONELY BIRD WITH BROKEN WINGS.'

SO I TURNED MY FOCUS ON THOSE WHO NEEDED ME.

I'LL FIX YOU, BECAUSE I CAN'T FIX ME.

I'LL SHOW YOU LOVE, BECAUSE I CAN'T LOVE ME.

AND MAYBE ONE DAY, I'LL FIND SOMEONE WHO LOVES
MY LOVE SO MUCH

THEY END UP LOVING ME.

Someone once described me as a healer. I scoffed at the thought. How could I possibly heal anyone? I can barely heal myself. But over time, I realized that there was truth there. It was true because I made sure to offer those who I love the simplest act of kindness that has become so undervalued in society—I listen. Listening is so vital, but we live in a time when someone is more eager to hear the sound of their own voice than to hear those who need to be heard. So, I always listened. I made sure to listen without the intention of responding, and because of this, I became the person people opened up to about their hardships.

I admired that about myself. I genuinely enjoyed it, too. I loved that I could sit down with a good friend or a complete stranger, and by the end of the discussion, they would tell me, "I'd never told anyone that before." There's a sense of safety in that statement, and I was honored to be the one to provide it. Lord knows I've had times when I needed it from someone else, so perhaps that's why I place such an emphasis on being that person for others. Regardless, it brought me peace to lighten the weight on their shoulders, and I'm truly happy to help carry out the words that are not often said. But it became tricky when the people spilling their emotions in front of me were men I loved, especially when the topic at hand was the women who still had a hold on their hearts.

This chapter is about one man who I loved in a way that was so crucial for my growth, because he inadvertently became an integral cog in the wheel of my personal development and self-worth. I found myself in familiar territory, but the outcome this time was exponentially different.

Yet again, I ended up loving a guy who had no intention of being committed to me, but I knew what this was—it was the Universe giving me another test.

Let's start from the beginning.

He caught my heart by surprise. Have you ever met someone for the first time, but when your eyes lock, it's almost like you've crossed paths before? Another life, another world, another Universe, who knows—but for whatever reason, someone who should be so foreign is so familiar. That's what happened with him. I always say time is irrelevant when the connection is real, because you can know someone for years, and still never feel as deep of a bond as someone you met last week. That's the magic of love and energy, and when you're lucky enough to experience it, you'll never be able to forget it.

This esoteric affair began with a modern twist that was no stranger to me. We met online.

No, we didn't find love on Tinder (that last experience I told you about was enough to delete the app for good), but I did first come across his presence on Instagram.

A mutual friend posted a photo over the holidays, and his smile instantly caught my attention. I gave him a follow because I'm aggressive like that, and before I knew it, we were in a full-fledged conversation in the DMs less than 24 hours later. It's a very millennial approach, I know, but what wasn't modern as far as today's standards was the depth of our conversations. See, our story isn't a particularly long one, but there's substance. Once that initial contact was made, we talked all day, every day for weeks about things that you don't normally talk about with someone you have yet to see face to face. He opened up to me about his rough childhood, and being raised by his grandparents because his parents were both incarcerated. I opened up to him about my fear of never being enough or finding the ability to love myself the way I should. We bonded over our dark past and dreams of using our misfortunes to create a positive space in the community. With a foundation like that, it was no surprise that we hit it off when we did actually meet.

The second I saw him, it was less of a, "Wow, there you are," and more of a, "Hey, it's you." It's always odd, yet fascinating, to be introduced to someone for the very first time and it instantly feeling like reconnecting with an old friend. And that's how it was with us.

Our first meeting was a bit of a whirlwind. I had invited him to my bar bash for my birthday, because I figured, what the heck? We'd spoken every day for weeks, and we had mutual friends who were going, so it seemed like a win/win. In an effort to gain some one-on-one time before being thrown in a scenario with all of my friends, we decided to grab lunch together prior to the party, and I was immediately drawn to him.

He was even more handsome in person, and he liked to talk a lot, but not in the *Jesus-Christ-will-you-shut-up* way. I don't know if it was the conviction in his voice or just the sheer enjoyment of hearing him spill random Google facts, but I sat there and ate my chicken salad with both ears and eyes intently on him. When it came time to say goodbye, I shyly extended an invitation to join me in running errands before my party, jokingly noting that I knew how much fun that sounded, in hopes of spending some more time with him before the big soiree. I was elated to see him jump in my car with enthusiasm and we were off.

He drove with me to my hairstylist's place and patiently chatted with us while I got my blowout, we went to the mall because he wanted a new shirt for the party, and then he played DJ for me and a few of my girlfriends while we got ready at my apartment. As weird as that may all sound, it felt so normal. Once I entered the bar, every single one of my friends' faces shot me a look like, "Who the fuck is this guy?" It was kind of hilarious. The problem with going to a function, let alone *your* function, with someone alongside you after being single for so long is that everybody will ask you about that person for a long time. And they did.

Regardless of being thrown in a situation that would make most guys sweat, he made a good impression that night, mingling with everybody while also making sure I was OK in my drunken stupor. As I mentioned, I'm not much of a drinker, so I quickly learned that having my birthday at a bar was the worst idea I've ever had. I was so sure that he probably would never talk to me again after seeing me so wasted that night, but to my luck, that wasn't the case. There was definite attraction on both sides, but the truth remained—he wasn't ready for anything serious.

This was nothing new for me. I was always getting guys who were fresh out of a relationship. In his case, he was on the mend from a 7-year relationship with a woman he thought he was going to spend the rest of his life with. So, not only was he heavily on the rebound, but he was also working through trust issues because she was unfaithful. I should've ran. I should've said, "Thank you for the amazing company and for telling the Uber driver to grab me McDonald's when I was too drunk to speak, but that's where it's going to end with us."

But did I? Of course not. And it wasn't because I was naively thinking that maybe this would be different. I just felt that feeling, you know? That feeling that you can't describe, but when you feel it and lose it, you begin to wonder if you'll ever feel it again with anyone else. At that point, I'd been mourning the loss of that feeling and facing the fear of never feeling it again every day, but then there I was feeling it again. And maybe it was selfish or stupid of me to hold on to it, but I wasn't ready to let it go.

So, I gave myself that little pep talk—"OK, Bru. He's obviously not ready for a relationship. Don't expect anything from him. Just be cool. Be fucking cool for once."

I tried to tread lightly. "I'm not ready for anything," he'd tell me, and I'd silently nod. He was on the receiving-end of heartbreak and dabbling with denial on anything related to his emotions, and I so badly wanted to tend to his scars with my love, but I had to stop myself. *It's not your responsibility to fix people, Bruna.* I had to stop sacrificing my well-being for the sake of others who wouldn't, or couldn't, replenish my love. So I kept a safe distance. Or, at least I tried, but love blocked logic, yet again.

We continued to stay in constant contact, which I secretly enjoyed because he almost always initiated it. But throughout our *hanging-out-but-not-dating* phase, I began to notice that other girls were entering the picture. *You knew this was bound to happen, Bru. He's in his liberated phase right now. Seven years. Let the man live.*

I tried. I tried to remember when I was newly single and where my head was at then, but no matter what explanation I gave myself, it always stung to know that there was another woman occupying his time in my absence.

One afternoon, he surprised me with a visit. Annoyed that I spent the entire day looking like a struggling artist who hadn't showered in weeks, I tried to rummage whatever I could to pull off the effortless-but-still-cute look (spoiler alert: I failed). I was a walking human capsule of fluttering butterflies, but that was nothing new. He always made me nervous. But the good kind of nervous. The excited nervous.

After exchanging some small talk and catching up, we began to talk about the real reason why he came over. He needed someone to listen. And who better to do that, right?

Again, my extremely comfortable couch served as a pseudo-therapist's chaise lounge as he began to open up old wounds. One by one, he peeled back the bandages as he went down memory lane, each thought visibly stabbing him with sharp pain as it was brought to the surface.

I sat there, looking at a man I was fighting the desire to love romantically, as he began to unravel in thoughts of her, listing all the things he misses about her and all the things that made him angry about her, but the anger was rooted in love lost. And then speaking of his late father, who he reaches for emotionally, but will physically never be able to touch again. In that moment, tears streamed down his face. There was no sound, just the image of him staring into his hands as the salt water left faint traces on his cheeks. I wasn't sure what to do. I mustered up whatever strength I had to keep my own emotions bottled up inside, and leaned over to hold him as he cried.

I'd be lying if I said it didn't hurt. My selfish desires hated that he was crying to me about another woman. My selfish desires wished a man loved me as much as he loved her that he found himself crying over my absence. My selfish desires wanted him to love me that much. But that was just my ego talking, and this was more than anything superficial.

You see, in that moment, I knew I loved him. I loved him so much that I held him as he wept. I loved him so much that I listened to him speak of fresh scars and bottled up fears. I loved him so much that instead of seeing a man who couldn't love me the way I wanted to be loved, I saw a man who needed love. Maybe it was silly of me to sit there and allow a man who knew the hold he had on me go on and on about the one he still longed for, the one who would never be me, but in that moment, that's what I felt I had to do. And there were many moments like that.

However, as selfless as I tried to be with his situation, that mentality that kept me pushing through those hard moments began to break down over time. I started growing resentment towards him. I started to question the sincerity of our friendship and the love we had for each other. He'd tell me he loved me constantly, but I knew when I said, "I love you, too," we were speaking different languages. Despite the laughs, long hugs, and heartfelt connection that we would have every single time we were in each other's presence, despite the memorable trip to the OC Fair, the movies at the park or the personalized tour of his hometown to paint me a picture of his childhood, he not only didn't want to be with me, but almost flaunted other women he was pursuing in front of my face. And, of course that made me mad. It made me mad because his actions never matched his words. It made me mad because he kept telling me he wasn't ready for commitment, but dated other women. It made me mad, because when I'd decide to pull away, he'd pull me closer.

One morning, I reached a boiling point. Not one to ever shy away from expressing my emotions, I explained to him my frustration. I told him that I don't believe him when he says he loves me, not because he doesn't want to be with me, but because even on the basic level of friendship, I felt like that love and respect wasn't being reciprocated. "I've learned a lot from you, and I hope you can say the same for me. But at the end of the day, you know I got you," I wrote to him. "No matter what, Bru has your back. I can't say the same for you. I can't help but feel like it's not really me you love, but how I make you feel... And while I love being that person for you, I have to stop and wonder at what cost to me?"

The response I got from him hit me like a freight train. In what felt like a dissertation on Bruna's flaws, he explained that everything I was feeling was a reflection of my own inability to fulfill myself, and that I seek love with the intent of getting love in return. He tore me apart in a way that I didn't expect, not from someone who claims to love you. But there was one line in particular that struck me to the core: "I now know what it is that is missing when it comes to a romantic desire for you... and that's your own lack of completeness... it's more apparent with you than with other women I've interacted with."

My own lack of completeness? The fact that I refrained from coming at him with a rebuttal that would go straight to the jugular after that statement came from a power greater than me. I kept the response simple, said "thank you" for illustrating why this would never work, and agreed that we should create some distance for the time being. I cried after that happened because...well, do I really have to explain why? I also cried because maybe there was truth to what he said? Am I incomplete? Had I spent the last two years working on myself, only to end up right back where I started? Did I fail this test miserably? In that moment, it felt like the answer was yes. But I prayed for clarity that night, and by the morning, I got it.

I can't explain the feeling that flowed through me the next day in any other way than this—I felt like magic. The heaviness that was in my chest over him had vanished, and I finally saw the actual test that was given to me. Everything that happened between us was meant to happen, because everything led to that conversation, which became my final exam. See, trying not to love someone who isn't ready wasn't my test, like I initially thought. I love who I love, even if it's extremely inconvenient. The test was never about him; it was all about me. It was a test on my self-worth, my self-love and my self-reflection.

Here was a man, an extremely hurt man, who maybe was projecting some of his pain on me, but whether he believed his words concerning my character to be true or not, I know that I always have the final say. I realized that nobody can tell me who I am except for me, and in all honesty, there was truth to what he said, which is why it hit me so strongly. I tried to fake my desperation for love, but he saw through it. While it is in my nature to be there for the people I care about, there was a sting of manipulation there (*oh, maybe he'll appreciate and need me so much that he'll begin to love me*). It was embarrassing, and I was mortified that the guy I had feelings for saw through all of it and called me out in a way that he knew would hurt me, but maybe that's the harsh slap in the face I needed to finally wake up.

Still, his approach was not rooted in love. There's a way to speak to those whose hearts you care for, no matter how ugly the message, which will still be received with respect and care. He was defensive and aggressive any time I spoke up about something that didn't align with his beliefs, and I knew that behavior was always about him and not so much about me. I was just a catalyst that was caught in the crossfire. I know who I am as a woman, a lover, a friend and a human being, and for that reason, I don't shy away from seeing my shortcomings, either. Therefore, no one can hurt me, because no one can define me and no one can tell me something about myself that I don't already know deep down inside.

As much as we understood each other, we also misunderstood each other just as intensely, based simply on the fact that we were at different points in our lives. I saw a lot of myself in him, and perhaps that's what kept me so closely tied to him, but the stage he was at in that moment was toxic. Despite his good heart and good intentions, his actions were selfish, and I didn't need to voluntarily sacrifice my well being in that situation. He got hurt, and now saw the world through a jaded filter that attempted to keep his heart safe. I knew that, but instead of practicing healthy boundaries, I went right to the front lines and said screw it.

I can't blame him for acting the way he did. I've been there. I've loved intensely and been crushed for it. I've been angry and pushed good people away. For all of those reasons, I was able to let it go and forgive. And that's when I knew that I grew from the woman I used to be.

He had once looked at my vision board and read one magazine clipping out loud: "Fall in love."

He turned to me, "Did you fall in love this year?" Maybe he was fishing to see if I'd say, "Yes, I fell in love with you," but I didn't say anything. The truth was I didn't fall in love with him. I very consciously stepped into love with him. I did, however, fall in love that year. I started to fall in love with myself, and I don't think I realized that until the moment he questioned my character and entire being. I'd waited so long to feel that feeling, and I made sure to note this breakthrough in my journal that night:

ONCE YOU REALIZED ALL OF THIS, YOU PROVED HIM WRONG, BECAUSE AN INCOMPLETE PERSON WOULD

CRIPPLE AT THOSE WORDS, BUT YOU TRIUMPHED! YOU
DON'T BELIEVE HE'S A BAD MAN. HE IS NOT ROOTED IN
EVIL AND DOESN'T HAVE MALICIOUS INTENT. HE'S JUST
BATTLING HIS OWN DEMONS... YOU CAN STILL BE
LOVING, RESPECTFUL, CARING, FUNNY & SUPPORTIVE
FROM A DISTANCE. BECAUSE OF THIS, I CAN SAY NOW
MORE THAN EVER, THAT I AM SO FUCKING PROUD OF
YOU.

As promised, we created some distance, and in an odd way, I felt free. But just as I was beginning to get my groove back, the craziest thing happened.

A girlfriend and I had planned a road trip to Lake Tahoe as part of my summer bucket list. I didn't really tell anyone about it, and if I did, I kept the location a secret. It came at the perfect time, because I had just gone through this emotional experience, and now I had the opportunity to recharge and get my mind right with some much needed relaxation by the lake. However, during day two of my getaway, after a number of Snapchats and tweets disclosing my destination had hit social media, I get a text from him.

"Hi, are you in Lake Tahoe?"

"Hi. Yeah."

"LOL the odds."

"What do you mean?"

"I'm about to be there, too."

Yes, friends. Of all the places in all the land, and of all the days, he just so happened to be in Lake Tahoe at the same exact time as me. And neither one of us knew we were going to be there.

Coincidence? Maybe, but I don't believe in coincidence.

The next morning, my girlfriend and I took a yoga class by our cabin. We were the only people there, so it was more like a private session. Our instructor Ingrid resembled Samantha from *Sex and the City* (Kim Cattrall) with an eight pack. To say she's fit is an understatement. She had a dominant energy, but was very sweet in her demeanor. While doing some stretches on our back and feeling the sweat begin to trickle down my forehead, she asked us in her strong Slovenian accent why we chose to vacation in Lake Tahoe. We gave her the standard, "Oh, just wanted to get away and recharge" answer. I turned to my girlfriend and whispered, "But it doesn't matter, because they end up here, anyway."

We giggled. Ingrid apparently felt left out.

"Secrets? Who are you trying to escape?"

"No, no secrets. Nobody, but it doesn't matter who we're trying to escape, because this guy I had a falling out with ended up here at the same time."

"Did he know you were coming?"

"Nope."

"Wow, that's very strange," she paused for a minute. At this point, we're sitting upright in a butterfly position and facing each other.

"Do you know what that means?," she asked.

Of course not, Ingrid, but I bet you're gonna tell me.

"Maybe this is someone you shouldn't try to escape."

Oh geez, Ingrid. I felt like I finally had it all under control, dammit!

"Maybe," I tell her. "But even if that's the case, the timing is way off for us."

"I'm sorry," she sweetly replied.

"It's OK. I know that what's meant for me will always be for me."

She nodded at my deep Pinterest quote, and then we laughed at our common grievance over the lack of hot men in Lake Tahoe, and united in our love for all the cute dogs.

Near the end of the class, she asked us if we'd be open to her doing some reiki on us during Shavasana.

I quickly gave her an enthusiastic yes, because I'm all about that life. I even explained to her that I considered taking classes to become a reiki master, and she confidently told me, "You will. I already sensed it." (Reiki is an ancient Japanese healing technique based on the principle that the person conducting it can channel energy into the patient by means of touch and help the healing process).

As I was lying there with my eyes closed, trying not to drift away into memories of the past or made up scenarios of what could become the future, Ingrid gently put her hands above my chakras, starting with my feet and ending at my head. Afterwards, she shared what she felt, and she blew me away.

"I felt like you had constriction in your throat," she began, which puzzled and intrigued me all the same.

"It was as if... you're a very smart woman, and you know what you want and how to express it, but there's someone in your life that no matter how you express yourself, they're just not understanding it. And that's frustrating you."

Well, damn, Ingrid. You just hit the nail on the head.

Although being in the same place at the same time, he and I never ended up getting together while in Tahoe, but the day before we left back to Los Angeles, he reached out to me. He first asked if I wanted to watch the stars with him that night, which I kindly declined, and then got to the actual point of his message— his car completely broke down and wouldn't be able to get fixed before having to head back to LA for work. After apologizing and acknowledging the tension between us, he asked if there was any chance that he and his brother could ride back with us. "I know you're not very happy with me right now and you have every right.. But I thought I would ask... I'm sorry, Bruna."

Now, most people would probably have just said, "Fuck no," including my friend who wasn't exactly his biggest fan and whose car we drove to Tahoe. None of my friends were exactly rooting for him anymore, because the string of events that followed after my birthday overshadowed that first impression, and I found myself constantly defending him, and myself for always helping him out. "You have such a pure heart, Bruna," they'd tell me, "and he just seems so manipulative. We just don't want to see you get hurt." I couldn't get mad at them for trying to protect me, but at the same time, I knew what I was doing. So, when it came to his favor, I said I'd talk to my friend to see if she'd be OK with caravanning it.

Regardless of questioning his intentions with me, my friend knew that I couldn't leave someone I cared about in this type of situation, so she said, "If you can make room in the car, I'm cool with it." I played Tetris with all of our stuff to see how much I could fit in the trunk, and to her surprise, managed to make two tiny seats open for them. While some may think that going out of my way to help him yet again was the wrong call, I'll never regret it. The truth is when I love you, I love you forever, and I'd do that for any one of my friends who found themselves in that situation. I'm not gonna leave you stranded hundreds of miles from home, and if I can save you some money and give you a ride, I will.

So, I told him, "You can ride with us. It's gonna be tight, though."

The next day, I jumped behind the steering wheel, and the four of us crammed into her Mazda 3 and took an 8-hour scenic drive down the 395 back to Los Angeles. We sang loudly to 2000s hip-hop, we talked about various topics, we listened to a few episodes of Serial, we took pictures, we enjoyed some McDonald's in the middle of nowhere, and we made memories I'll never forget.

Once we got back to my house, I went in my room to grab a jacket from my closet and he met me there. He came up behind me to tell me how much he appreciated me and I turned to meet his arms around me. We just hugged for a long time, and he told me, "I know you may not believe me, but I'm so grateful for you. You saved me again."

Sometimes I may sacrifice more than needed for those who others may deem undeserving, but I lead with my heart, and I'd like to believe it's stronger than it may seem.

Our connection may not have resulted in some intense romance, but it's become easy to see that we were meant to serve crucial roles in each other's lives and the bond we share will never die. Over the years that passed after that experience, we each went our separate ways while building a strong friendship. He began dating someone else, and although I always thought I'd dread the day I'd have to see him love another woman, it actually made me happy, because that's how it was always supposed to be. I was just grateful that he chose a woman who wasn't intimidated by our past or our friendship, because I would've hated to have to lose our friendship. His harsh and abrasive approach softened over time, a testament to his own healing, I presume, and he ultimately would become one of the few people who always made sure to check on me and my heart.

Meanwhile, I continued my ongoing journey to finding myself again and learning how to make healing myself a priority. I knew there was a lot of truth in the things that he'd said to me, which is why I took so much offense. He called me out, and regardless of what his motives were or if there were variables that added to why he reacted the way he did, I knew it was on me to own up to my own denial.

In life, we meet a lot of mirrors. These are people who cross our paths to give us direct reflections of things we may not acknowledge about ourselves. He was one of my mirrors, and he showed me parts of myself I didn't want to see. A dating and relationship blogger admitting that she sucks at dating and doesn't even love herself? I was already dealing with imposter syndrome for the mere fact that I was giving advice even though I was single, and all of that on top of it would just throw me over the edge.

But, ignoring it doesn't make it untrue.

Growth is accepting all of you—the good, the bad, the ugly, the pretty, the embarrassing. I wasn't doing that, because I was afraid, but he wasn't going to let me get away with it. For that reason, I will always remember him as the one who pushed me, because he forced me to see that the love I always searched for from other people was within me the whole time.

And with that, I let go of the comfortable denial that I was swimming in, and forced myself to face who I truly was.

5

THE ONE WHO TOOK MY INNOCENCE

THERE'S A PAIN THAT LINGERS JUST BENEATH THE SURFACE.

I'VE BECOME GOOD AT HIDING WHAT HURTS.

PRETENDING IT DOESN'T EXIST, AND ALL IS FINE.

SMILE ON MY FACE, BUT A WAR IN MY MIND.

IT'S TROUBLING TO BE IN THIS BATTLE, I KNOW THIS MUCH IS TRUE.

BECAUSE WHO'S TO TELL WHO WINS, WHEN IT'S YOU VS. YOU?

THE DARKNESS CREEPS IN. SLOWLY THEN SUDDEN.

TEARS ON YOUR FACE AND YOU'RE UNSURE WHY, BUT YOU SUCCUMB TO IT ALL AND BEGIN TO CRY.

THE SALTWATER DRIES, AND YOUR BREATHING SLOWS.

OPEN YOUR EYES, AND LET IT GO.

HEAD TO THE BATHROOM, AND WASH YOUR FACE.

LOOK IN THE MIRROR, GET RID OF THE TRACE.

Let That Shit Go

TAKE A DEEP BREATH, HEAD OUT FOR THE DAY, AND
TRY YOUR BEST TO MASK THE PAIN.

They always tell you to fall in love with your best friend. What they don't tell you is that sometimes, you see certain sides of your best friend that you didn't even know existed until romance enters the picture.

He was always there. My best friend's brother, and a good friend of mine, too. He watched me navigate through the hurdles of heartbreak throughout my teenage years, courtesy of his own best friend mistreating me, silently sighing when verbal abuse was thrown my way, and feeling caught in the middle when he'd witness infidelity but couldn't tell me about it because that would be breaking guy code. Regardless, he knew the pain I was in. Perhaps he knew more than I did, and so he'd offer me words of comfort and meaningful hugs. He became my best friend. He was the nice guy, the guy that all the girls in high school liked as a friend but didn't necessarily jump at a chance to date, which I'm sure wasn't his preferred situation, but it deemed him trustworthy. He was sociable and shy, sweet and funny. The type of guy that got along with pretty much everyone. He was the one you'd think would work out in the story of my love life, but instead, he hurt me in ways I never thought possible.

It was near the end of my sophomore year of high school, and I was trying to connect the dots on why my first experience at prom wasn't all it was cracked up to be. I guess it depends on who your date is. Instead of feeling beautiful and taking in a night of dancing and memories, I spent it fighting with my boyfriend (his best friend), who constantly knew just what to say to make me feel like I didn't deserve to breathe the same air as he did (we'll get to him later), before ultimately parting ways for the rest of the evening.

I had spent the night at my best friend's house (the sister of this chapter's, um, Casanova), and woke up in the morning to him getting in from a long night of post-prom partying himself as a last hurrah for their senior year. As I lay in bed, watching TV while his sister slept in the other room, he snuck up behind me to lie down. This wasn't necessarily peculiar behavior, because we'd been good friends for over three years at this point, and spent countless time together, but something was different that morning. Whether there was still a bit of liquor in his system or he was just tired of playing coy, he made it clear that friendship wasn't all he wanted from me.

Despite going to the same prom and hanging around the same group of people, our recollection of that night was very different. In short, he actually had a good time, and during that conversation, with him behind me, talking to my back as I continued to watch TV while listening to him, he surprisingly said, "Turn around so I can kiss you." I laughed.

"Yeah, OK. You're not going to kiss me."

"Turn around."

In an attempt to call his bluff, I turned around, and was quickly met with the fact that he wasn't bluffing at all. He kissed me passionately, as if he'd wanted to let that kiss happen for a long time, and I was caught off-guard by the shocking revelation that I wanted that kiss, too. Once we realized what was happening, we pulled away. What were we doing? No one could know about this. After all, his sister was my best friend, and his best friend was my boyfriend (albeit, a shitty boyfriend, but still). We tried our best to tuck that kiss away and move on from it, but it just wasn't possible. It opened the door to the next two years of my life.

We attempted to keep our budding romance under wraps. I had officially ended things for good with my boyfriend, a breakup that should have happened years prior. Meanwhile, I tried to convince myself that keeping this from my best friend, his sister, was the best thing to do. I wasn't sure how she'd react, and I didn't want to stir the pot before knowing what we wanted to come out of this. Regardless, we found time to meet up in secret and explore whatever was evolving with our romance. It was beautiful. I felt like I had finally found a guy who appreciated me and wanted to treat me the way any woman wanted to be treated by a man she loved, and the fact that we had years of friendship under our belt made me feel confident in allowing him in, despite my troubled past with guys, because he respected me. He wouldn't hurt me.

At one point, we knew we wanted to make this thing official and just deal with whatever backlash we might get, which meant letting everyone in on our little secret. Some people were excited, and as expected, others were infuriated. His best friend, my ex-boyfriend, threatened our lives out of anger, because he felt betrayed, and maybe I should've felt bad, but in all honesty, I didn't. If he wanted to keep me, he should've treated me better. What did break my heart, however, was the response I got from his sister.

I was hoping, that as my friend, she would be happy to see two people she loved find happiness with each other, but that scenario never saw the light of day. She called me a slut, and let me know our friendship was over. I blubbered through tears on the other line that I just wanted her to be happy and wished she could feel that way for me, but as we all know, you can't control someone else's feelings. So, I had to live with her decision. You can imagine how awkward family dinners and get-togethers were after that. I'd never been disliked by my boyfriend's family, so this was new (and horrible) territory for me. I wasn't sure how to manage it all, and at times I'd wonder if it was worth it, but ultimately, I was with someone who made me smile, and I wanted to allow myself the ability to enjoy that, even if no one else was going to.

It never got easier, though. Friendships were divided, and his family wasn't sure whether they should cater to his sister's sense of betrayal or celebrate the happiness of their son. It was us against the world, or so it felt, and although hurdles kept being thrown our way, we didn't let it dim our love, so we chose to flourish it. We spent a lot of time together, we went on dates and spent days in, I'd sneak out of my house to meet him in the middle of the night just so I could see him, and he'd sneak into my backyard just to give me a kiss through my bedroom window. It felt like forbidden love that you wanted to root for, but soon enough, the fairy tale aspect of our relationship was severely trumped by reality.

I began to notice that he had some vices I wasn't a fan of. His relationship with Mary Jane proved to be quite the committed one, and his drinking became more frequent. It wasn't anything shocking. He was 19 years old, and all of his friends were about that life, and while I had my own judgments at the time over those recreational hobbies, it wasn't *what* he was doing as much as *who* he'd become when doing them. When he was high, it was like trying to have a conversation with a bucket, and when he was drunk, well, we'll get there.

I had never smoked at that point, so I didn't understand the appeal. In an effort to compromise, I told him I'd try it with him if he would promise to cut down on the smoking afterwards. He agreed, so I got high, and instantly hated it. I was extra paranoid the entire time; the clock moved way too slow, I was having cough attacks and my throat felt like baby dragons were blowing fire down my esophagus. And, as you probably already assumed, my plea bargain didn't hold up. He continued to smoke every chance he got, and instead of fighting about it, he'd just lie. "I'm just tired," he'd tell me. I was offended at how dense he thought I was. At one point, it got to a level that I just couldn't take anymore, and I told him that if he kept smoking, we couldn't be together.

Oh, baby Bru. Ultimatums never really work, especially if you don't stick to your guns.

He said he'd quit, and I believed him. At least, I tried to believe him, but I knew deep down he was still smoking behind my back. I gave him so many opportunities to be honest with me, but he wouldn't, so I went to the drugstore, bought a home drug test kit, and gave it to him.

"You're not smoking, right? So this shouldn't be a problem."

"But I'm around people who smoke," he tried to argue. Again, how cute of him to think I was that big of a fool. But the joke was on me all along, because when he tested positive for marijuana, I didn't do anything about it. Not cute.

"So what? Are you going to break up with me now?" he asked.

I should've, but instead I just cried, and to this day, I couldn't tell you if I was crying because he called my bluff or because I felt stuck in another relationship that fed me so many lies so easily.

At the time, lying about smoking weed seemed like the absolute worst thing that could happen, but it was the gateway lie to much deeper problems. There was an aggressive side to him that I had never seen before. I didn't know what to do with it, and I never knew when it was going to come out, but when it did, it made sure to overshadow any good memories we made together.

The first incident happened on what would've been any ordinary day. We were hanging out in his room with his former best friend's (my ex) brother, just talking and messing around, when he decided that he wanted to play wrestle with me. We tussled and laughed and I played along, hoping he wouldn't tickle me to death like he usually did, but something went off in him, and we weren't playing anymore. I couldn't tell you when the switch happened, but suddenly I was lying on my back with his hands grabbing tightly around my neck. Neither one of us were laughing, and it was getting harder to breathe. Our friend didn't know what was happening, and

I kept wanting to yell for him to get off me, but between trying to catch a breath and all the tears that were coming down my face, I couldn't get a word out. I don't remember what finally got him off of me, but upon seeing the reaction on my face, all he could say was, "What? We were just playing."

The second instance happened late one night after drinking with one of his best friends. I got a call that he was too drunk to drive, so I lied to my dad about a girlfriend of mine being in trouble and in need of me to go pick her up. I got in my car to go get him, and knew at first glance that this was not going to be a pleasant ride home. He'd been drinking some 80 proof vodka from Poland all night, so his interpretation of reality was jaded, to say the least. He had taken his puppy, a black and white rat terrier, with him to play with his friend's new dog, but apparently, the other dog decided to get frisky, and that didn't sit well with him. Belligerent as all hell, he explained how he caught the other dog having sex with his puppy, and that pissed him off, so much so, that he punched a dent into the glove compartment of my car as a reaction to telling me the story.

There he is.

I tried to remain calm, even though I was angry that he did that and also fearful of what he could do next. When we got to his house, I held his puppy while trying to aid him in walking up to the door, but at one point he decided to turn and lock his arms around me. It wasn't a hug. It was the type of hold you put on someone you're trying to contain. With the dog between us, his grip kept getting tighter.

"Stop, she's not gonna be able to breathe," I told him, referring to the dog that was now getting squeezed between us.

"If she can't breathe, neither can you," he told me, and squeezed even tighter. Mission accomplished. I couldn't breathe, and just like the other confrontation, I just cried. But this time, I managed to say something.

"Get the fuck off of me," I yelled. And surprisingly, he listened.

I went into his house to see his sister still up, making a late snack in the kitchen. We still weren't on speaking terms, but she looked alarmed, seeing I had been crying and her brother acting the way he was. I needed my friend in that moment, but she was long gone.

"He's drunk. I have to go," I simply said, and got out of there as fast as I could.

The last altercation took the longest for me to fully comprehend and accept. His aggressiveness made appearances when it came to sex, too, but not so much during the act as much as demanding it, and sadly, no additional substances were needed for that side of him to show. Two specific situations come to mind.

The first was when he got mad at me for not wanting to have sex in the bathroom at the beach in Catalina Island. We chose to take a day trip to the island along with two other couples who were friends of ours to have some fun, but his anger at my refusal to just get it in the moment he asked for it put a damper on the mood. He was so mad that he stopped speaking to me.

The tension was palpable, and instead of enjoying the waves, beautiful beach and gorgeous weather, I was busy faking a smile to everyone else while being guilted into feeling like I was a bad girlfriend for not handing over my body the moment it was called upon.

But that was nothing compared to the memory that still haunts me, the time that will forever live in my brain, the moment that made me realize I was sexually assaulted by someone who disguised himself as my protector, my lover, my best friend.

It was just another day at his house, and his entire family was home. He casually asked me to go to the bathroom with him, and I did. I didn't think anything of it at first, but then he closed and locked the door behind us. Red flags started to prop up, but again, I tried to convince myself that nothing crazy was about to happen. Plus, his entire family was home.

He made it clear that he wanted to have sex. I made it clear that I did not.

"Everyone is outside," I said.

"So?" he replied.

"I really don't want to right now," I pleaded.

"C'mon. I need it," he said.

I should have made my way past him to the door to get out, but I didn't. I should have refused to let him take my clothes off, but I didn't. I should have punched him and told him this is not how you treat someone you love, but I didn't.

Instead, I froze. I still remember the feeling of the cold tile on my bare back. I turned my face, because I couldn't look at him, and like a dead animal, I just stayed stagnant while he had sex with me. All I remember is the yellow hue on the walls from the bathroom light, and the pain of every thrust because my body wouldn't produce the natural lubricant it needed to help make this experience enjoyable. I didn't want it. I knew that. My body knew that. He knew that. But it happened, anyway.

After he finished, I went home and showered for what felt like days. The shower always felt like my safe haven. It always managed to camouflage my tears, because even when I was alone, I felt ashamed to cry. I remember digging my loofah into my skin, trying to scrub his touch off of me. But even then, I didn't realize what had just happened. I figured—I did what was expected of me. I was his girlfriend, he wanted sex, and therefore I owed it to him, regardless of how I felt. My heart breaks for the little girl inside of me who thought that way.

I stayed with him throughout everything, and it wasn't until many, many years later that I realized what really happened to me, because I was conditioned to believe that his behavior, even though it innately felt wrong, was just a guy being a guy, and I was probably overreacting. But that's not true at all.

When you think of rape, you don't think of having sex with your boyfriend. You picture walking down a dark alley and being assaulted by a stranger. But rape comes in all shapes and sizes. Sometimes it comes in the shape of someone you love and trust, and somewhere along the way, I was made to believe that sex is assumed in a relationship, and therefore doesn't need to be consensual. But it does. It absolutely does.

There is no clear-cut picture of what sexual assault looks like, other than there being a lack of consent, and even then, people argue about what constitutes as a yes or no. I didn't give my consent in various ways, verbally and otherwise, yet knowing how society works, I would be the target of blame in the situation, because I "let" it happen. And you know what? I "let" it happen a lot of times in my life.

Guy friends who crossed the line, men who wouldn't take no for an answer so I'd give in just to get it over with, strangers who felt entitled to grab at my body in a crowded bar and would proceed to act out if I didn't reciprocate their interest, male associates who would make inappropriate comments. Somehow it was always my fault. *You should've dressed more modestly, you shouldn't drink so much, you should've just said no, you should've fought back...*

Should've, should've, should've.

Instead of focusing the problem on the perpetrators, we make blanket excuses (boys will be boys!), and pinpoint the blame on the victim—every, single, time. How many girls have to lose ownership of their bodies, their sanity, their free will, their self-respect, before we realize that we're not taking care of the root of the issue?

We're just trying to live our lives, but apparently, that's asking too much.

So, yes, maybe I "should've" done a lot of things differently, but he should've behaved better. He should've been taught better. He should've learned that there is absolutely no situation that grants you an automatic "yes" from any person and a refusal of acknowledging that is unacceptable.

The crazy part is even when the light bulb went off and the veil was lifted, I couldn't be mad at him, because I genuinely believe that he didn't know better. We don't have proper sex education for men, and that affects everybody. Sure, there are instances when you don't need a lesson on to know it's wrong, and some people engage anyway, but what about all of the in-between? The situations where someone can easily discount their actions because it wasn't a clear-cut yes or no, and therefore, they interpret it as a yes and everyone shrugs their shoulders and lets it go?

The trauma that lingers with survivors of sexual assault is deep; so deep that survivors themselves hardly even understand it. I went 15 years without knowing that I was assaulted, because even I thought that type of behavior was normal. How many other girls are also blindly excusing their assault?

It wasn't until our two-year anniversary that I decided to break up with him. Instead of celebrating the special day with me, he was at his friend's house getting high on drugs that were a step up from weed, and I was stuck wondering why I was in this relationship anymore. I called him and told him, "You're a horrible boyfriend. I don't want to be with you anymore." He didn't think I was serious, hung up on me, and then called back a few hours later, asking, "Are we still going to the movies tonight?"

I know I put up with a lot of bullshit, more than I should ever even admit to, but one thing that's true with me is when I hit my boiling point, there's no turning back. It didn't matter how many tearful voicemails he left me, or flowers on my doorstep, or cards on my car—I was done.

Once I saw the different sides of him, the ugly sides, I couldn't look at him the same way. The guy I considered my best friend was gone. The man I saw a future with was gone.

Shortly after our breakup, we ended up at the same house party. One of his best friends got into my car and asked me to drive around the block so we could talk. He was trying to save face for his friend, and I just listened to his little speech, but I was already over it. Plus, no one knew what he was really like as a boyfriend, and it almost felt pointless to try and explain that to anyone, because it was such a far cry than the man they all knew him as.

And then his best friend told me something that I never expected to hear.

"You know you were his first, right?"

I didn't believe him at first, but his face reassured me that he was revealing the truth. Stunned, I let this new information sink in, but never did anything with it.

Looking back, I guess we each ended up with a piece of innocence from one other. The only difference was he handed his to me by choice, and mine was taken from me by disillusioned force.

Sharing this story is probably one of the hardest to do for obvious reasons. The fear of being judged or ridiculed, along with the fear of how those who know this man may react, stopped me from typing these words many times. But again, silencing the experience doesn't make it disappear, and when the #MeToo movement began, I realized how important it was to share.

It wasn't because of the vast amount of women who'd suffered sexual assault coming forward and speaking up, although it was a very moving experience. It was because in spite of so many people coming together to be a voice for what can feel like a very voiceless experience, there were still those who chose to rank what constitutes sexual assault. There was a hierarchy forming, as if one person's experience and subsequent pain could ever be paralleled to another's. It broke my heart to see some women, who were survivors themselves, discredit other women's experiences because it was different than their own.

Yes, I understand that the trauma I've held on to from my boyfriend forcing sex from me is nowhere near the trauma caused by someone who was attacked by a stranger or threatened with death or molested by a family member, and I would never equate the two as the same.

However, the pain that comes from any interaction where you feel as though your voice is unheard and your body is not yours is still valid. I found myself struggling with how to deal with the emotions that arose, because it felt like my anguish wasn't worthy. "It's not like he tried to kill you, Bruna," I told myself. So? That still doesn't make it OK.

Sometimes it seems as though people try to paint a picture of what rape and sexual assault looks like, and it's one hell of an ugly, disturbing, heart-wrenching image. Anyone's experience that deviates from that scene is instantly overlooked. But what we fail to understand is it's always that image, the only difference is it's not always visible to the naked eye, but felt and tucked away internally.

It makes sense that people would categorize such horrendous actions in such a way. It helps make them feel safe, because the ugly truth of the matter is that rape and sexual assault happens to so many people daily, and by opening the spectrum of what it looks like, we'd then have to admit that we've experienced it ourselves, and then we'd have to deal with everything that comes with it, and it's not pretty.

I talk about him doing all these drugs and how much it pissed me off, but the truth is I was suffering from the biggest drug of all—denial.

As you witnessed, denial followed me for years in many forms and became my gateway to many hurtful perceptions of who I was and what I deserved. Regardless of it taking so long to see what this relationship really was, I'm so grateful for that clarity.

Because now, I can take all of the pain that had been drowning me from trauma I didn't even realize I'd endured, and let it go.

6

THE ONE WHO TRIED TO BREAK ME

I HAVE FINALLY REACHED THE OTHER SIDE, WHEN THINGS BECOME SO CLEAR.

NO LONGER JADED BY YOUR CHARM OR THE FALSE PROMISES THAT I'D HEAR.

I SEE WHAT YOU ARE.

A SAVAGE IN THE GAME.

YOU COME IN, WREAK HAVOC, AND THEN LEAVE ALL THE SAME.

SO BROKEN, I THOUGHT YOU WERE IT.

"COME BACK AND FIX ME, COME BACK AND FIX THIS."

BUT IT WAS NEVER YOU I NEEDED.

YOU ONLY BROUGHT PAIN.

SO HURT YOURSELF, HURTING OTHERS KEPT YOU SANE.

I was so young. The fresh-faced 14-year-old who was always so eager to enter adulthood was now getting ready to tackle the hurdles of high school, and I was pleasantly surprised with the fact that I was already gaining the attention of older boys. The girl who was always made fun of as a kid was suddenly the girl who was making boys' heads turn, and my self-absorbed teenage self couldn't deny the satisfaction that came along with it. I don't know if it was because my boobs were bigger than the other girls or if they could smell my fresh innocence from a mile away, but whatever it was, Bruna became a hot price item, and it didn't matter to me whether the attention was ill-willed or not. I was just happy anyone noticed me.

Of course, the one I chose to invest my energy and reciprocation into was the worst of the bunch, and so, instead of being one of those girls who got to sit next to her boyfriend at lunch and make-out or the girl who would get flowers on Valentine's Day, I was the girl who dealt with serious drama on a continuous basis. Not the best introduction to the dating world, I know. Trust me, my self-esteem issues remind me all the time. But alas, my relationship with this guy my freshman year of high school was when I began my first "real" relationship (read: the relationship was bullshit in retrospect, but I can't deny the very *real* shit I experienced while in it).

He wasn't the guy anyone pictured me with. In fact, he was probably the last guy anyone saw me dating, ever. I was the teacher's pet who had great grades and was friends with everybody. I was always sociable and sweet, and although my eyebrows were a mess, I was still considered pretty cute. And he, well, he was trouble. Not only was he older and um, *more experienced*, than I was in various ways, but he wasn't the most academically inclined guy you'd meet. I struggle to think of what it was that made me cling to him for so long. It wasn't his looks. It wasn't his sincerity or great personality, because those two factors were non-existent. It definitely wasn't the way he treated me. Oh, and did I mention he was gang affiliated? *Sigh.*

Yeah, I fell for the whole bad boy thing. I was so naive, I didn't really care to think about what any of that really meant when I got involved with him. He was pretty much any parent's worst nightmare for their daughter, but all I knew was that he had his eyes on me, and since I was a novice in the dating game, he didn't have to try too hard or say much for me to be completely smitten.

It was more than that, though. I dedicated two years of my life with this guy, and ultimately, I think the reason he managed to pull that off was that he provided me with an escape from the world I was living in. The world that dealt with court hearings and packed bags to dad's house every weekend. The world that started to question if love really existed and if their divorce was my fault. The world that I wasn't sure I belonged in. So instead of facing reality, I created my own alternative reality by living somewhat of a double life. I was the girl who would never turn in a homework assignment late, but would sneak out of her house to meet up with gang bangers, because one of them was her boyfriend. That became my reality.

Because this was my first time really dating anyone, I didn't know what was acceptable and what wasn't, so he got away with a lot of shit he shouldn't have, and not just with our relationship, but with the hold he had on my self-worth. I was a very fragile and impressionable young girl, and he didn't waste any time trying to claim whatever dignity or confidence I had as his own. I remember nights when he'd message me just to tell me what to wear the next day and how to do my hair, or to complain about my makeup. No matter how hard I tried to look good for him, it was never enough. Instead, he'd look at another girl right in front of me, and ask, "Why can't you look like her?"

As if I wasn't insecure enough at that age, when you don't know what the fuck is happening with your body and you're still outgrowing your weird and ugly stage, he made sure to bury whatever self-esteem I had in the dirt. And it wasn't just with his words. No, sir. His actions always spoke levels higher than anything he could say to me.

Despite living just a few streets away from me, we rarely saw each other for the simple fact that he "didn't want to see me," so our time together was mainly spent during passing period at the end of the day, when he'd travel from his alternative school to our school, or the few nights I'd sneak out to meet him and his friends for a drive to Azusa Canyon, where they'd smoke weed and drink Alize and I'd just sit there and stick out like a sore thumb (side note: that was one thing I was proud of myself for. I never succumbed to peer pressure. Thanks, D.A.R.E).

I hated Mondays, not because it was the first day of the week, but because Mondays were always the days I'd hear about what he did over the weekend with other girls. The cheating was a constant thing, and he'd always resort to his famous argument—"I have needs." Remember, he was older and no noob to the dating game. I was a virgin, and for over a year, I didn't give it up to him, despite everyone's preconceived notion that I had because I was dating *him*. The minute I became his girl, people assumed I instantly spread my legs open, and that's not an outlandish thought, because he wasn't exactly the type of guy who'd wait. But I wasn't that type of girl, and although I thought I loved him, I was still skeptical (and scared) to go all the way, and no words were able to charm his way into my pants.

So, I held off, and he managed to always throw it back in my face as an excuse when he was caught being unfaithful. We'd have our usual fights, I'd cry like my life was over, he'd come back and apologize in some half-ass way that seemed genuine to me at the time, tell me he loves me, and the vicious cycle was back in motion, because my denial of the actual situation would fog up my logic and somehow subconsciously spin my train of thought to believe that it really was my fault. *He has needs, Bruna, needs that you're not giving him.*

I remember one day, his brother sent me a message on AIM asking if we were still in a relationship. I was puzzled by this question. Doesn't everyone know that the Tupac lyric in his AIM profile is dedicated to me? Regardless, I told him yes, and asked why he felt the need to wonder that. He proceeded to tell me that another girl was over at the house, and they were all shacked up in his room. That all-too-familiar feeling of my heart sinking into my stomach came back, but it didn't sit there long enough to stop me from figuring out what the fuck was going on. I was done trying to go to him for answers, so somehow, I found this girl's number, and there I was, a freshmen calling this junior girl I didn't know to ask her why she was at my man's place. She claimed to not know about me, but didn't deny their fling, and in an effort to prove it to me, she suggested we three-way call him to see what he'd say.

Remember three-way calls? Oof.

I'm not sure if that was really her way of establishing innocence on not knowing the status of our relationship, or if she was just cruel and really wanted to stick it where it hurt, but at one point, I was staying silent on the other end, swallowing my sobs and trying to maintain my composure as I heard her tell him, "I miss you," and he'd reply, "I miss you, too." I couldn't keep my lips shut any longer and I blurted out profanities at him while trying not to cry before hanging up the phone on both of them. You'd think that was the end of it, right? Nope. After some time, my brain somehow chose to ignore the thousands of red flags, and he managed to weasel his way back into my life yet again. And unfortunately, into my pants.

One night, we went to a house party, and to my unpleasant surprise, two girls he had cheated on me with were also in attendance. One, who was triple my size and also gang affiliated, was in the bathroom with me and a friend of mine along with some other girls, and I don't know what came over me, but as I watched her apply her makeup, with her bud leaf tattoo peeking out of her lower back as she leaned forward, I said, "Aren't you the girl who fucked my man?"

Everyone's eyes widened, probably because they thought my death was about to happen right there in this random person's bathroom, but before anything could really pop off, my friend rushed me out of the room, which I'm grateful for because that girl could've smushed me like a bug. The bravado lingered, so much so that it clouded my judgment, and for whatever reason, that was the moment that I felt was the right time to sleep with him for the first time.

I remember telling him I wanted to have sex and although he was puzzled and surprised, he obviously didn't question it. When I was younger, I imagined my first time being a magical experience, with candles and rose petals and a man who treasured my body and reaffirmed that fact with every gentle touch that was followed with a soft kiss. My actual first time was the exact opposite.

We went into another bathroom in the house, locked the door, I took out my tampon (yes, I chose to lose my virginity while I was on my period, because why not make this experience worse than it already is?) and then I jumped up to sit on the bathroom counter to experience an underwhelming few minutes of sex for the first time. I remember trying not to get blood on his white and baby blue Marc Ecko hoodie. I remember the metallic smell mixed with the putrid fragrance of the forgotten throw up in the toilet. I remember the look in his eyes, which at face value seemed like a look of passion, but I knew that wasn't what it really was.

It was almost like he was sad, because even he knew that he shouldn't have been the one to do this. I remember my heart racing, not because of our love making (you couldn't even call it that), but because I felt like I lost myself. I knew in that moment that I wasn't doing this for the right reasons. I was having sex with him so that every other girl he slept with under that roof saw him go in there with me. But even more than that, I was having sex with him in hopes that it was the secret ingredient to finally get him to love me.

In the two years that we were off and on, we had sex three times. Three. And each time was absolutely horrible. There was the first time that I just so pleasantly illustrated above. There was the second time, in which he stopped midway and said he'd just finish himself off in the bathroom and left me lying there naked, confused and wondering if I'm absolutely repulsive. And then there was the last time, when he got off (I never did, FYI), and proceeded to quickly put his pants on while telling me, "This never happened."

But even then, even after such horrid experiences that would no doubt become part of very deep issues that would remain in me for years to come, they still couldn't claim the unfortunate title of my darkest moment, both in this relationship and in my life.

For years, I heard his voice when I thought of my insecurities. I heard his judgment when I looked in the mirror and felt unsure about who I saw reflected back at me, wondering why I look the way I do and not like some of the other women I see. It was his face I'd see when I thought of the way I used my body to try and have a man love me. But none of that compares to what happened during our relationship on a November night, just before the holidays.

A mutual friend invited me over to his place for a pre-Thanksgiving celebration, and told me my boyfriend said he'd be going, too, so that was enough reason for me to try and find a ride and an excuse out of the house. Before I left, in an effort to plant the seed, I texted my boyfriend that I was excited to see him. He was definitely surprised, but not in the way I'd hoped. His response hit me at my core: "Why are you going? If you're going, I don't want to go."

I asked him why, and reminded him that we hadn't seen each other in weeks. He said, "I don't care, I don't want to see you."

Was this the worst thing he'd ever said to me? Sadly, I couldn't bet on that, but at that moment everything that had accumulated up until that point overwhelmed me, and I did something that less than a handful of people in my life know ever happened.

With tears streaming down my face, I went into my bathroom and locked the door. I sat on the toilet seat cover, opened the drawer next to me and pulled out the sharpest pair of scissors we had. I opened them as wide as possible to get a better grasp, and I let the blade pierce the skin of my inner wrist and cut right down the vein. For a few moments, the physical pain overshadowed my emotional pain, and that was the initial goal, but it didn't last. It never did. The cutting was just a temporary fix to what felt like a permanent wound, and I couldn't tell you what I thought that made it seem like a plausible solution, but that was my way of dealing with things at the time. I wish I could say that was the only time it happened, but that wouldn't be true.

I remember confiding in my best friend about it. At the time, she was the only person who knew what was going on, and she became the only person who got me to stop. After another rough night one Christmas Eve, I ran over to her house to celebrate with her family and hopefully become distracted from whatever I was feeling. I walked in wearing an oversized gray hoodie and large, black sweat pants per usual. She took one look at me and said,

"Let's go to my room. You can borrow something." My family was never big on holiday celebrations, so this was new territory for me.

While trying to find something more appropriate to wear for the occasion, I was met with a startling discovery that broke my heart. She showed me her arms, cut up much worse than mine ever were. In that moment, I realized that I'm the one who gave her that idea, and I felt disgusted with myself. I cried over her pain and over the revelation that I had a hand in someone I love hurting themselves, and through our love for one another, we promised to both never do it again.

In retrospect, I feel like that was God's way of showing me how hurtful my lack of self-love and care was. I believe everyone we meet is a reflection of ourselves, and so, it almost seemed as though God was like, "Bruna, you may not see how much you're worth, so I'll show you how painful it is to see someone you love so much hurt themselves the way you do, so you can get a glimpse of what I'm feeling."

Another mirror.

No matter how many times I try to put that moment behind me, I'm reminded of that night every time I look at my arm. The faintest scar that is barely visible to the naked eye is all I see, but now, instead of viewing it as a moment of weakness, I look at it as a reminder that even in my lowest of lows, I was still able to move forward. I'll always have a strong emotional response to this memory, and I can't fight the tears that escape me now as I type this, but it's not because of shame or guilt. I lived it. I felt pain and I felt useless to a degree that I hope no one ever has to feel, and unfortunately, I chose to deal with it in a manner that wasn't the healthiest. The tears come from a place of sympathy, because the memories seem so distant and almost surreal now, as if they were lived by another human completely, and I begin to wish that I could go back and hug that little girl. I wish I could tell her that it's not her fault he treated her this way, and that she didn't have to hurt herself so much to take away the pain in her heart. I wish I could've wiped the tears from her cheeks and let her know all of the beautiful things about her. I wish I could have told her what a tremendous woman she was going to become.

My toxic relationship finally reached its ending point not too long after. Two years of my life was spent devoted to a man who couldn't even do me the common courtesy of being a decent human being, so I was pretty ruthless when it came to breaking it off. He'd show up at my house in the middle of the night, crying to me about everything that happened, and you know what I did? I laughed in his face. I laughed without even having to think about it, because that was my natural and genuine response to this guy. How dare you come to me and cry crocodile tears over me leaving you when you did nothing but treat me like a disposable toy from the day you pursued me. As expected, it didn't take long for his sadness to turn to spite. *You better watch your back, because I put a hit on you in the street. If I can't have you, no one can.*

Nothing ever happened, and although there's not a minute that I regret closing that door, the mystery of his behavior throughout it all always left me wondering. Why? Why treat a good girl who only tried to love you so horribly?

The closest conclusion I'd ever get was one offered by a mutual friend of ours. He would always give me the biggest bear hugs when I was crying at school in an effort to cover my face from everyone else, because he knew I hated letting people see me so vulnerable. He told me, "Bruna, he wanted to show people that he could get you. And then he wanted to show people that he could break you."

He may have gotten me for a lot longer than he should have, but regardless of what happened during that time in my life, he will never have the satisfaction of being able to say that he broke me.

All I did was try to learn how to love someone, and unfortunately, my first "teacher" taught me more of the opposite. I pity him. How broken must one be to try and break another person's spirit, let alone the spirit of someone who only wanted to love you?

I may not be able to go back to that young girl in the bathroom and stop her from being so cruel to herself, but I can share my story and spread awareness to the fact that physical harm, although it may seem like the only way out sometimes, is *not* the way to process your pain.

My first relationship was with a boy who couldn't love me because he refused to love himself, and instead of recognizing that, I let his hatred and toxic energy spill over to me and affect the way I viewed myself and my worth. That is way too much power to give to someone who has proven to be so reckless.

And with that, I let all those lies of what "love" looked like go.

7

THE ONE WHO TESTED MY GROWTH

Sometimes the best things in life are not carefully created

But stumbled upon and then cultivated

Sometimes a fiery passion can burn out quick

But a slow-burning flame can be the one that sticks

Sometimes you realize you shouldn't fall in love

But willfully step into it with hope and trust

Sometimes the answer is right before you

But you're too busy looking back to see the truth

Sometimes you see a friend in a different light

And realize everything you'd ever needed was there in plain sight

One of the things they don't tell you about self-love is that it's just *one* part of the process to creating a healthier relationship with someone else. Becoming whole on your own, and finding peace in yourself and happiness in solitude, is to help you attract the right type of partner, however, that doesn't magically make all of your flaws and insecurities vanish once you get into a relationship.

Inviting another person into your life is an entirely new dynamic with fresh obstacles. Suddenly, traits that you thought weren't a part of your identity anymore begin to rear their ugly head and you're like, "WTF are you doing here? I thought I got over this." But sometimes those closest to you become a trigger, and you find yourself facing an entirely new level of challenges. The only difference is that now, all of that self-work you've done thus far has hopefully trained you to properly process and analyze your actions objectively, and more importantly, also helped you attract someone who's down to go through the trenches with you so you can reach the other side relatively unscathed.

And that's what I realized with him.

Even after all of these failed attempts and interactions with men, who, in some form or fashion, affected the way I viewed and approached love, I was still blind to just how much of an impact it all had on me. Perhaps I was too busy focusing on others who needed healing as a distraction from having to heal myself. Or perhaps I hadn't met the right person to put me in a comfortable position to allow myself to heal, because I can do endless self-work alone, but would I be able to put that work to use when a man entered the picture. Whatever the case may be, I found myself in a situation that forced me to shed the insecure and paranoid skin I was in, and I'm not sure I would have been able to do that without him.

This romance, like the ones before it, caught me by surprise, and while there were a lot of moments that seemed like unfortunate deja vu, there were also some very monumental lessons and areas of growth that felt like reassurance from some higher power telling me that I was exactly where I was meant to be.

He was no stranger to me. In fact, we'd been friends for over five years at the time, and while the chemistry was palpable to anyone who witnessed our subtle glances and smiles to each other from across the room, that was as far as it got for a very long time. He was always involved in an on-and-off relationship throughout the years that I'd known him, and I was cliff-jumping from one situationship to another—most of which have been described to you in this book—so we weren't really able to explore the connection that came naturally to us for quite some time. It worked to our benefit, though, because we were able to use that time to solidify the foundation of our friendship without any expectation or preconceived notions as to what our interaction could be.

Our correspondence for the first few years was always casual. I'd see him at gatherings with mutual friends, or go out to support his singing career, but that was the extent of it. He was a handsome man with kind eyes, a genuine smile and the type of body that seemed to be sculpted by Michelangelo's very own hands, but I didn't realize the depth of his beauty until I was able to get a glimpse of his soul. I couldn't tell you what sparked our desire to get to know each other on a deeper level, but once the conversations began to dig beyond the surface, they were hard to turn off. We'd text each other random questions late at night about the Universe, religion and human behavior, just because we were so intrigued by each other's thoughts. When everybody else was fully immersed in a dream state, our minds were buzzing with esoteric questions like, "What did you learn about God that nobody else taught you?" or "If there was another version of you that existed in a parallel universe, and you were able to sit down and ask them one question, what would it be?"

We shared a deep appreciation for literature and art. We'd swap book recommendations and discuss the central themes and messages, visit used bookstores in search of hidden gems, and stop at poetry lounges to get inspired for our own art. We'd get lost in time just sitting on my couch, watching movies or listening to old music that proved to be timeless. Or, my favorite, having more out-of-this-world conversations that ranged from philosophical rhetoric to peeling back the layers of our own respective histories. It was all very organic and honest, and for the first time in maybe ever, I felt like I was getting the treatment I so often give to others. See, it's nothing new to delve into deep conversation with me, however it was new that I was the one in the hot seat during most of our interactions. I'm usually the listener, but with him, the spotlight was on me and I was given the healing. Normally I'd feel apprehensive in such situations, but surprisingly, I dove head first, which I can only assume meant I needed it more than I realized. He created such a comfortable energy for me to unveil the parts of myself that I'd often kept in the dark, and his willingness to listen without judgment was a gift I didn't even realize I'd been missing.

In the beginning, I made sure to keep my proper distance. After all, in my mind, he was just my (extremely attractive and intelligent) friend, who, for all I knew, had a girlfriend. However, I later found out that his relationship had come to a (seemingly final) end, and I began to notice subtle hints of this progressing into something more than just two platonic friends enjoying each other's company. The hugs lasted a beat longer than normal, his hands always found a comfortable home around my body, his feet always seemed eager to rub against mine underneath the blankets on my couch, and with every touch, no matter how minimal or grand, the heat rushed through my body and my heart began to thump like a caged animal trying to break free. It was in those moments that I was so grateful for my dim lighting, because I could only imagine how flushed my face looked, and I wasn't quite ready to let him know what a hold he had on me. Despite his clues of interest, though, I waited. I waited for him to make the big move and act on what we both felt but refused to fully acknowledge. I waited, waited, waited...but nothing happened.

Then one night, we reconvened on my incredibly comfortable couch to watch *Shutter Island*, a Leonardo DiCaprio thriller that he insisted I see. Once we got the mood set up for a movie, he took his now-usual position of spooning me from behind, while I tried to maintain a regular breathing rhythm to not give away the nervous excitement that he brought out in me. He was right, the movie was great, even though I correctly predicted the big plot twist at the end, and after it was over, I turned to face him, and we continued to discuss the film in the dark through heavy eyelids. It was late. I could tell he was trying his best to stay awake, but one blink lasted longer than usual, and he began to doze off next to me. I watched him for a few moments, which I understand can sound a bit creepy, but it wasn't. I just wanted to take him in.

Well, that's a lie. What I really wanted to do was grab his face and kiss him all over, and normally, I wouldn't have any qualms in doing so, but every time I'd come close to going for it, I'd get too shy and back out. He briefly woke up to shift his body, "Sorry, my elbow was right in your face," he laughed. I was worried that he'd realize he was falling asleep and say it was time for him to go, but he wasn't in any rush to leave. He never was. I smiled, and then shifted my body to get even closer to him.

"Bruna, if you don't do this now, you may never do it," I told myself. Flashes of the previous five years filled my mental space. See, the truth is, I'd felt something for this man during our entire friendship, but continued to write it off as just a silly crush. However, there were distinct moments sprinkled throughout that time that hinted my feelings were more than I was willing to admit—the surprising stings of jealousy when he got attention from other women, the immediate excitement when I'd see him, the twinge of sadness when I'd say goodbye, the longing to know what it was like to be the woman on his arm.

So, as he began to return to his reverie, I leaned in and kissed him on the lips. He sleepily began to kiss me back, but once he realized what was happening, the kisses got deeper, the embrace was passionate, and our limbs had no desire to let go of the messy maze they'd created. Once I thought to come up for air, the first thing that escaped my lips was an apology. "I'm sorry, I had to," I told him. I wanted him to know that I didn't mean to possibly ruin our strengthening friendship by now bringing physical intimacy into the picture.

"Don't be," he told me. "I've wanted this for so long."

I'd always wondered if he felt what I felt all those years, or if I was alone in this unspoken attraction, so hearing those words said aloud put my heart at ease and also inspired a little dance inside my chest. I melted back into his arms, and we continued to embrace each other like two lovers who had been separated for far too long, and while I enjoyed every moment, I needed to pump the brakes. Straddled on top of him, I sat up with my hands on his chest and let out a sigh. He grabbed my hands, and, knowing what I was saying without saying it, told me, "We can wait." At this time, I was still going strong with my choice to steer away from noncommittal sex, and he knew that. Overjoyed with the fact that he understood and respected my stance, I nestled myself back down onto his body, and continued kissing him until we fell asleep with our lips refusing to part from each other.

His schedule made it difficult to see each other regularly, and he wasn't exactly the type of guy that was prompt with the calls and texts, which didn't help in silencing my insecurities. Nobody knew of our blossoming romance, which meant playing it cool when around mutual friends. We weren't quite sure what to make of everything, so there wasn't any need to further complicate the matter by inviting outside voices for their two cents. It wasn't easy, but at times, it was kind of exciting. During a friend's birthday dinner, I became quite weary that he was going to show up with someone else. I don't know why I feared that. I guess I just didn't know if that late-night encounter meant as much to him as it meant to me, and with his ex always coming back in the picture, I felt it necessary to brace myself for yet another discouraging greeting with her on his arm. But to my relief, he showed up alone. Since he was late, he sat at the only available seat on the other end of the table. We'd share a few glances here and there, but that was it. And then, while checking my phone, a text from him popped up. "You look really nice tonight," he wrote. I looked up and smiled at him, and proceeded to be filled with giddiness from his undercover admiration for the rest of the night. At the end of dinner, I went and sat next to him, and we quickly fell down the rabbit hole of conversation. The only thing that broke our concentration on each other was our friend calling to us. "Uhh, are you guys ready?" We looked around to see the entire table had already gotten up to leave, and that was the perfect illustration of our relationship. When we were together, we were always in our own little world. It was beautiful and I never wanted to leave.

"I want to try something," I told him one night, as we sat on my couch. "It might seem weird, but I've always wanted to do this with someone I felt comfortable with."

His interest was piqued. I giggled at his sexual assumption.

"I know your face. If I saw you from across the room, I'd know it was you, because I'd recognize your features," I explained to him. "If I thought of you, I'd have a picture of you in my mind, because my memory can draw your physical appearance as a reference.

"But what if I couldn't see you," I asked him. "What would you look like to me? What would you feel like?"

"So," I continued, as he silently followed along in my hypothetical story, "I wanted to know if you'd be OK with me just touching you, with my eyes closed." He had absolutely no problem with that, and I was once again reminded at how much I love being around a man who doesn't hold my sometimes weird and random antics against me.

"Could you take off your shirt?"

I didn't *really* need him to take off his shirt, but with such a gorgeous body and the ability to touch more skin, it seemed like a sin not to ask.

The mood was set—the fireplace was lit, we were sitting in candlelight and my favorite classical music was playing. He sat up on one side of the couch, with his legs sprawled across the length of the sectional, and I sat up in between his legs facing him.

"OK," I told him, "I'm going to start with your toes."

I closed my eyes and extended my arms back to find his feet. Slowly, in gentle squeezes, I began to explore his toes, the balls of his feet, the arch, and began moving up each leg. His shins, his knees, his upper thighs. When I got to the groin area, I paused. "I'm going to stay away from this area for now," I said, still with my eyes closed but with a smile that said everything I was thinking. I heard him laugh and could easily picture the grin on his face. Instead, I moved to his core, letting my fingers dip into every crevice of his muscles.

I let out a whisper, "Jesus Christ."

Hey, there was no denying this man's physique. I continued with his arms, touching his shoulders, biceps and forearms before interlacing my fingers with his and massaging his hands. I moved closer to him, and as if I was going to hug him, I lightly began to caress his back. I could feel the goosebumps rise on his skin and his breath on my neck. My heart started racing. With his face right in front of mine, eyes still closed, I let my fingers outline his face; from his brow bone down to his cheeks, my thumbs grazing over his eyes, which were now closed too, and then his lips. Every sway of my thumb against his lips brought me closer, and finally, I cupped his face in my hands and went in to kiss him again. He kissed me back with such fervor that I fell back on the couch. He held me like he never wanted to let me go, and I was grateful for that, because I never wanted him to.

It would have been nice to allow myself to completely surrender to whatever this was and just play out the fantasy of what this could be for as long as possible, but that's just not me. I needed to talk about what we were doing. I needed to hear his take on everything. After all, there was a friendship at stake here. A friendship that I valued very much, and although I'd already fallen pretty deep into whatever we were doing, I knew that I'd rather claw my way out now than later if that was going to have to be the case.

"I'm scared," I told him as he sat next to me at my apartment one sunny afternoon. "I don't know what we're doing here, and I don't want to ruin our friendship in the process."

I continued, "This is not to say that I regret anything that's happened so far, and that's also not to say that I won't continue to make advances at you, but I want to make sure we're on the same page."

He nodded. I proceeded. "I like you," I said to him. "And not in a, 'Oh, he's cool, I like him,' way. I like you–like you." I felt like a schoolgirl getting ready to pass my crush a note to see if he liked me, too.

"I like you, too," he interjected. I smiled, picturing him passing me the note back with the "yes" box checked off. I continued, "But when I like someone, I get tunnel vision, which is good and bad...I respect you and care for you, I'm not going to have you out here looking like a fool."

"What do you mean?" he asked.

"I mean that there's no other guy out here right now that can tell you he's experiencing the same moments with me as you are."

His face softened with a smile.

"And I want that same respect from you," I added. "I know you're fresh out of a relationship. I know you need time to do whatever you need to do. But if you want to pursue other women, I need you to communicate that with me. I don't want to be out here thinking that what I'm experiencing with you is exclusive to me, when there are other people getting that same privilege."

"I can do that for you," he simply said, and proceeded to tell me that there was no one else. This was the first time I didn't shy away from telling a man what I wanted and what I felt like I deserved. I'd always been made to feel that by doing so, I'd come off needy or clingy, but after so many years of pretending to be OK with things that didn't sit well with me, I was over it. If being assertive and making my needs known marked me as someone who was asking too much, then maybe you're offering too little.

"How about we take a vow that no matter what we do, we put our friendship at the forefront, and if we feel that it's going to hurt that, we don't do it," he told me.

This was so easy, I thought to myself.

When it came time for him to leave, we lingered at the steps of my apartment complex, and for the first time, he made the initial move to kiss me. I don't know if it was the reassurance of knowing that he was the only man in my life or just the comfort that had been formed up to this point, but there was a certain shift in his energy that told me he felt safe, too. We shared one of those hugs that stopped time but also seemed like an eternity. In fact, my neighbors called us out. "All right, there are kids who live here," they joked.

"I can't say goodbye," I laughed back. I was only half-kidding.

That entire experience made me think—perhaps men needed that same security that women often ask for? Perhaps he still had somewhat of a guard up because he thought he was one of many or was fighting the same fear I was? Maybe what men and women look for in a relationship isn't that different at all?

The casual meetings and late-night rendezvous on my couch continued, and some even turned into sleepovers. There's something very powerful about being able to comfortably sleep next to another body. I fit into him like a puzzle piece, and I'll never forget the morning after our first sleepover together when—while we were both in that asleep-but-somewhat-awake state—he faced me and brushed the hair out of my face before kissing me softly on my forehead. He didn't know I noticed that, and he'll never know how many times I replay that moment in my mind. Whenever he stayed over, I'd accompany him with his morning routine, which meant waking up at 6 a.m., meditating, reading, writing, visualizing and doing daily affirmations. I definitely don't consider myself a morning person, but I loved every moment of it because it was with him.

While I cherished our nights in and early mornings together, I didn't want to be typecast as the girl he just chills and talks to late at night on the couch, so one day I was feeling extra courageous and asked if he'd go on a date with me. I was nervous for his response, but was relieved when he responded, "Of course!"

Years prior, we'd spoken about my love of sunsets and talked about going to the beach and experiencing it together at some point, but it had never happened. With that in mind, I decided to pack us a picnic and head to one of my favorite beaches in Malibu so we could finally watch the sunset together. I had been feeling a lot of anxiety beforehand for numerous reasons—I wanted everything to go smoothly, I was worried he'd change his mind and say he couldn't go after all, and most of all, because my insecurities kept whispering that I was wasting my time swimming in this gray area with him. I knew I needed to talk this out with him again. I was ashamed of my need for constant reassurance, which I can only imagine would become bothersome on his end, but I felt like it would be better than the alternative, which is letting my mind wander and come up with horrible scenarios as conclusions to my unanswered questions.

While sitting on my huge beach towel, admiring the pastel horizon, our sandwiches, the music playing from his speaker and the multiple engagement photos happening around us, I said to him, "So, we told each other we would make sure we're always on the same page, but we never discussed what page that is."

"Yes we did," he told me.

"No, we didn't," I retorted, and stayed silent as a cue that I want him to tell me what page he's on. He got the hint.

"Well," he said while mentally preparing whatever he was going to say next. "I think it's clear that there's a connection here, and our chemistry is something we've both felt for a very long time, and I'm happy that we're able to explore that."

And then, the "but" came.

"But," he continued, "I just got out of a very long relationship, and I'm in no way ready for another right now. I don't want you to think that anything between me and you is contingent on things with her, but I do feel it's unfair of me to jump into anything right now without having some time to get myself right."

It's not necessarily what I wanted to hear, but it wasn't a surprise either. I knew that's where he was, and as his friend first, I had to respect that. After the sunset, we carried all of our stuff back up the big hill to the car, and it was off to the second destination.

"Time for dessert," I winked, knowing that it wasn't what I made it out to seem. During the hour-long car ride back, we both opened up about our childhoods. I told him about my troubled relationship with my parents after the divorce, the dark moments of my past and the mentality that evolved from it. He told me about his father's absence, the admiration he had for his mother's work ethic, and the plan he instilled in himself as a young boy to become the type of man he valued. As I drove down the windy roads of Malibu, I was also navigating through the windy roads of his past. Roads that I knew not many had traveled. At the same time, he was navigating through the lonely roads of my past. Roads that not many cared to travel. I was grateful for that.

We finally arrived at Cheesecake Factory, an idea that sparked from one of our conversations where he mentioned that he'd always wanted to try as many cheesecakes as he possibly could, so I figured why not start now? We shared a strawberry cheesecake while talking about soul mates, the idea of past lives and our own skeletons in the closet. Once we got back to my house, we let the adventures of the day wind us down into each other, and we just silently sat together, embracing one another and enjoying each moment we had experienced that day. Before he left, I expressed that I had one more surprise.

"Another one?" he said with animation.

I grabbed my blue journal, a journal he'd always eyed and questioned in the past. "I wonder what's in there," he'd always ask me, hinting at his fascination with my thoughts. That made me feel special that he cared enough to know what filled my quiet moments. Maybe he wondered if he was part of those thoughts? I wonder if he knew just how many of those thoughts he owned. I handed it over.

"This is your journal," he said.

"Yep. And now it's yours to read."

"Wow. This is the biggest sign of trust that you could ever give me," he said with such sincerity.

I smiled back.

I was nervous, to say the least, at what his response would be to all of my innermost secrets. He'd read about things I hadn't really told anybody else. He'd read about other men. He'd read about himself.

While looking down at the journal in his hands, I began to say, "Don't…," but then simply said, "Never mind. If you do, you do."

"I won't," he told me.

"You don't even know what I was going to say."

"I know, but I won't."

For the next week, every thought that ever crossed my mind was in his hands, and my paranoia was increasing by the minute. Yes, I wanted to be completely open and honest with someone. I wanted someone to see the not-so-pretty sides of me and still accept me. However, as twisted as this sounds, I think a part of me was using this as an attempt to push him away. He'd read something and think, "This girl is nuts," and then boom. I'd feel validated in my assumption of, "He left just like everyone else," when really it was just my self-sabotage doing what it does best.

However, he didn't do that. When he came over to give it back to me, he complimented certain pieces he'd read, and thought it was one of the greatest things I could've done for us. "I wish more people were able to be that honest," he said. "I'd like to give my journal to you one day, so that I can reciprocate, but I feel like there's not enough in there yet."

The thought alone made me smile.

After expressing my fear that he'd run for the hills after reading all my flaws on paper, he told me, "I'd never run after seeing the deeper layers. That's the best part. I appreciate you opening up to me so freely. This is a true connection."

And even with that, I couldn't avoid the part of me who made me question everything. I was very much outside of my comfort zone with him. I was completely submerged in the gray area, a place I absolutely hated, and while I continuously tried to reassure myself that everything was going to be OK, because he wasn't just any other guy, he was my friend who had my best interest at heart, it was still hard to rationalize what we were doing when my anxiety would take control. It was very difficult to silence my mind, even though I was well aware that it has a track record of working against me. Whispers of, "He doesn't love you like you love him," or "If he really cared, he'd be with you," or "You really believe he thinks about you as much as you think about him?" would cloud my judgment, and more often than not, I found myself fighting this silent war of trying to convince myself that my heart knew better than my head, even though I wasn't entirely sure that I truly believed that. The fact that we couldn't speak or see each other regularly because of our schedules only aided in my insecurities about what this was.

"Of course I want to call you and see you and do things together all the time," he once told me. "But I have to stop myself from doing that, because this would undoubtedly turn into a relationship, and I'm just not ready for that yet."

One day, I felt like I'd hit a wall.

I needed some reassurance from something greater than me, greater than him. So I did what I'd only done once before—I asked the Universe for a sign. I once came across a post by self-proclaimed "spirit junkie" Gabrielle Bernstein that illustrated how to ask the Universe for a sign. I'd used her tips when I was torn between whether or not to quit my corporate job and leap into the unstable self-employment life, and it worked, so I thought—why not test it out again? That morning, I wasn't sure if I was going down the right path with this man. My gut (or what felt like my gut, but perhaps it was my insecurity) was urging me to just shut it down. Shut everything down. Tell him this isn't working because we want different things and then push him away so I'd never have to even entertain what could be because there's nothing there to feed the fantasy anymore. But that's what I'd always do, and maybe, this was different. Was the lesson to stand up for what I wanted (a stable relationship with clear labels) or was the lesson to stop always trying to be in control and just go with the flow?

So I asked the Universe: "Dear Universe, if going down this unclear path with him is of the highest good for me, show me in the sign of an owl." Why an owl? Because I knew I didn't own anything that was an owl, and it's not something you see too often, so I knew if I did see it, it was for a reason. After putting my request out into the Universe, I got ready to go on a hike to clear my mind. While waiting in the car at a red light, something told me to look up. I glanced up, and my eyes laser-focused to something in the distance that read, "O-W-L" in big white letters. "You've got to be shitting me," I said to myself. I was amazed, and confused, because why the hell does it just say OWL in the middle of the street? Once my car moved, I realized it was a banner for the Hollywood Bowl, but from where I was parked, the Hollywood and "B" in Bowl were perfectly covered. I got my sign, and I got it fast. That gave me a sense of reassurance. During my hike, a stranger stopped me and said, "I'm sorry to bother you, but you're absolutely gorgeous." I refrained from my usual sarcastic response (*I'm sweating balls and have no makeup on, are you sure?*) and simply said, "Thank you, that's very kind of you to say." He proceeded, "Are you seeing anyone?" Technically, no. We didn't have a label, but my heart was spoken for. "I am," I said.

One of the first thoughts that went through my mind after giving that response, was a friend's voice saying, "What the heck. You know he wouldn't have said the same thing if a girl asked him that."

It's true. I don't know that he would've reacted the same way if he was in a similar situation, but ultimately I realized that my actions are not based on what he would or wouldn't do. They were based on what felt right for me, and in that moment, telling another man that I was available felt like a lie, because I was emotionally attached to someone else. When I met with him again, I told him about asking the Universe for a sign and seeing it instantly. The smile that formed on his face told me that he wanted this, too. The timing may not have been ideal, but this was something special nonetheless.

Regardless of not being a couple or not knowing where we stood romantically, the imprint he left on my life was undeniable. He brought me closer to God without either one of us realizing it. Never being much of the religious type, I realized that my spirituality was rooted in a type of faith that I hadn't completely understood but so badly wanted to embrace, and he created an open and safe space to help me maneuver through that journey in whatever way felt right for me.

He also helped me mend my relationship with my father. I don't think he realizes that, but because there were so many similarities between them (seriously, it was kind of weird), I was reminded of the things I loved about my father, before things got complicated and our bond became a distant memory. Like I mentioned, I didn't like to speak about my dad with people too much, because it always got me emotional, but I opened up to him about everything, because he made it easy, and the connections I kept seeing between him and my father made me subconsciously try to figure out how we can fix whatever we had broken.

Like my father, he was kind and patient. He was often quiet and listened more than he spoke. His love for books reignited that familiar feeling of being a little girl with my dad, excited to share my thoughts on the latest piece of literature we'd both read. In fact, one of the first things he told me when we began talking was, "Bruna! I keep forgetting to tell you—there's a poet I love and he's Lebanese! Have you heard of Kahlil Gibran?"

Have I?! My dad always kept his books around. This sparked my interest in rereading some of his work, which also led to extending a proverbial olive branch with my father. I messaged my dad asking if he could send me a few copies of his Gibran books, because, although I could go to any bookstore and cop my own, I wanted the copies that my father owned. He was very pleased with my request, and when my mom came back from Lebanon with five Gibran books in her bag, I was surprised to see that my father penned me a note and stuck it inside *The Prophet.*

DEAR BRUNA,

LONG TIME AGO, I BOUGHT THESE BOOKS FROM THE ARCADIA PUBLIC LIBRARY FOR FIVE DOLLARS, ONE DOLLAR EACH, GO FIGURE. AFTER READING THEM, I FIGURED I HAVE MADE THE BEST DEAL OF MY LIFE. THEY WERE PRICELESS. I FELT COMFORTED, RELAXED AND SATISFIED. THEY ARE SIMPLY WRITTEN, MYSTIC AND BEAUTIFUL. AND NOW AFTER ALL THESE YEARS, YOU SOMEHOW CALLING ME AND ASKING ME ABOUT THEM. I AM GLAD YOU DID, BECAUSE I AM SURE THEY WILL HELP YOU A LOT. I THINK YOU WILL LIKE THEM, AND I HOPE YOU DO LIKE THEM AS MUCH AS I. GIBRAN IN HIS BOOK THE PROPHET IN THE SECTION ENTITLED "SELF KNOWLEDGE," SAYS, "YOU WOULD KNOW IN WORDS THAT WHICH YOU HAVE ALWAYS KNOWN IN THOUGHT," AND HEARTS I MAY ADD. I THINK THE BOOK DOES JUST THAT, IT EXPRESSES SENTIMENTS WE HAVE ALL KNOWN BUT HAVE BEEN UNABLE TO COMMUNICATE THROUGH WORDS. HOPE YOU ENJOY!

LOVE,

DAD

The tears were endless after reading that, as if my dad was telling me something to hint at the reason for the lack of communication in our relationship, too. And as if I wasn't emotional enough, I turned over the index card to find that he also penned one of Gibran's pieces called "On Children."

AND A WOMAN WHO HELD A BABE AGAINST HER BOSOM SAID, "SPEAK TO US OF CHILDREN," AND HE SAID:

YOUR CHILDREN ARE NOT YOUR CHILDREN. THEY ARE THE SONS AND DAUGHTERS OF LIFE'S LONGING FOR ITSELF. THEY COME THROUGH YOU BUT NOT FROM YOU, AND THOUGH THEY ARE WITH YOU YET THEY BELONG NOT TO YOU. YOU MAY GIVE THEM YOUR LOVE BUT NOT YOUR THOUGHTS, FOR THEY HAVE THEIR OWN THOUGHTS. YOU MAY HOUSE THEIR BODIES BUT NOT THEIR SOULS, FOR THEIR SOULS DWELL IN THE HOUSE OF TOMORROW, WHICH YOU CANNOT VISIT, NOT EVEN IN YOUR DREAMS. YOU MAY STRIVE TO BE LIKE THEM, BUT SEEK NOT TO MAKE THEM LIKE YOU. FOR LIFE GOES NOT BACKWARD NOR TARRIES WITH

YESTERDAY. YOU ARE THE BOWS FROM WHICH YOUR CHILDREN AS LIVING ARROWS ARE SENT FORTH. THE ARCHER SEES THE MARK UPON THE PATH OF THE INFINITE, AND HE BENDS YOU WITH HIS MIGHT THAT HIS ARROWS MAY GO SWIFT AND FAR. LET YOUR BENDING IN THE ARCHER'S HAND BE FOR GLADNESS; FOR EVEN AS HE LOVES THE ARROW THAT FLIES, SO HE LOVES ALSO THE BOW THAT IS STABLE.

I remember I couldn't wait to show him the note from my father, and the books he sent me, and when he finished reading the card, he was astonished. "Your father just said everything I've always believed to be true. That's crazy. I really hope I get to meet him one day."

Never knowing my dad, he was always able to offer objective insight to help illustrate my dad's perspective, without taking sides. Also, because his demeanor reminded me so much of my father, his presence in my life reminded me how much I missed my dad, how much I loved so many parts of him, and how alike we actually are. Perhaps that's what hurt most when it came to the anger and resentment that I placed on my father—trying to hate him for things that have happened was in some way a form of hating myself. And I didn't want to hate myself. Some of the things I love most about myself are direct reflections of him, and it becomes that much more apparent as I grow and stabilize into the woman I was always meant to become.

This man who initially came into my life as a friend, who was in the background of so many other failed attempts of love, snuck into my heart and not only showed me love in so many different ways, but also provided me the willingness to put my pride and ego aside so that I could rekindle one of the most important loves of my life. I can't thank him enough for that.

He put me in a position that required me to let go of the superficial love I'd been blindly participating in, and really delve into unconditional love—the type of love we were all meant to practice from the beginning, before we let fear, pain, ego and insecurity make us believe that exercising that type of love was unrealistic. He pushed me to accept love that is simple and pure without question. The type of love that was perfectly summarized in a Bible verse that has now seemingly become so saturated that we've forgotten the importance of its meaning.

"LOVE IS PATIENT, LOVE IS KIND. IT DOES NOT ENVY, IT DOES NOT BOAST, IT IS NOT PROUD. IT DOES NOT DISHONOR OTHERS, IT IS NOT SELF-SEEKING, IT IS NOT EASILY ANGERED, IT KEEPS NO RECORD OF WRONGS. LOVE DOES NOT DELIGHT IN EVIL BUT REJOICES WITH THE TRUTH. IT ALWAYS PROTECTS, ALWAYS TRUSTS, ALWAYS HOPES, ALWAYS PERSEVERES. LOVE NEVER FAILS. BUT WHERE THERE ARE PROPHECIES, THEY WILL CEASE; WHERE THERE ARE TONGUES, THEY WILL BE STILLED; WHERE THERE IS KNOWLEDGE, IT WILL PASS AWAY. "

1 Corinthians 13:4-8

What I felt was a deep connection and genuine love, as sincere and cosmic as it was, still wasn't enough to solidify an actual relationship, though. It's hard to get on the same page as someone when you're on entirely different chapters, and no matter how much I wanted to conveniently forget that he was in a different place than I was when it came to committing to a relationship, I was faced with that harsh fact time and time again.

One night—after months of yo-yoing between embracing the love we shared and trying to create safe distance as to not brew false expectations—I cuddled up onto him and let my eyelids get heavy to the rhythm of his chest rising and dropping. I could've stayed silent, but my heart had other plans. Once I mustered up the courage, I told him, "I don't want to take a step back anymore."

He was confused.

"What do you mean?"

"I never wanted to take a step back," I explained. "I did that because I felt like I needed to protect myself."

"From what?"

"From falling too deep into something that doesn't exist. But pretending and holding back hurts more than that."

I was hoping for something, anything, to tell me that he was in the same place as me. A smile to show his excitement at being able to act on our desires again. A passionate kiss like the ones he used to give me that told me everything he never said. But I was met with none of that. Instead, he reaffirmed that this was the beginning of the end.

"The time we spend together means a lot to me, but acting on things will make this something that it's not, and the last thing I wanna do is play with your emotions."

I stayed silent. A million things ran through my mind, but nothing managed to come out of my mouth.

Minutes continued to pass. He finally asked, "What are you thinking about?"

"Everything," I responded.

After what felt like a lifetime of silence, I simply said, "We want different things," a line that seemed obvious but was never actually said out loud.

He nodded, and once the silence became deafening, he said, "I better go home."

He went to pick up his overnight bag, an accessory that used to bring me joy when I saw it, because I knew it meant I'd be sleeping next to him for the night. But not that night, and maybe not any other night after that.

We hugged, but even those embraces lost their intensity over time. One of the things I loved most about him was that no matter the case, he always held me with care, and was never quick to let go. This time, though, he could barely keep his arms around me. His energy shift over the last few months were hard to ignore, and it was clear that he was letting go in more ways than one.

Without a word, not even a goodbye, he left.

I instantly began to cry the second I closed the door. I buried my face into my hands and mourned the loss of something that gave me so much joy and hope. Yet even with my sadness, my chest felt light. Was that a sign this was the right move or had the reality of what just happened not yet sink in?

I couldn't tell if it was strength that kept me from completely falling apart, or if I was just numb to what I had just experienced, but I knelt down to pray and ask for support, anyway. All I could get out were four words: "Please stay with me."

I couldn't sleep that night. I canceled whatever meetings I had the following day and spent the better part of my morning going through waves of hysterics. One minute, I was feeling peace and acceptance, and the next, I was struggling to breathe between loud cries that came from my soul.

I knew he meant well. I knew he did what he thought he had to do to not hurt me, but he broke my heart anyway.

As I've mentioned, he was just like my father, which also meant he was great at loving me from a distance, believing his care for me was implied and therefore never feeling as though exerted effort was necessary. And, even though I knew he did that on purpose, because he didn't want to start something he wasn't sure he could commit to, the fact that he claimed to love me but was OK with pushing me away, and leaving space open for another man to come in and do what he refused to do, hurt all the same.

Just like I did with my father, I had continued attempting to pull the love and affection out of him, because I knew it was there and I wanted to feel it, but the reality is that type of love should be given freely and in abundance. I knew better, but I guess I was so used to that limiting belief that I didn't even really notice what was going on until long after it was over.

Still, I had to remind myself that it wasn't all about me. There were two people involved in this scenario, and once I was able to stop making myself the center of attention in this *whatever-you-want-to-call-it*, I realized that I was dealing with a man who was still picking up the pieces of a failed relationship while also trying to solidify himself and his life. I had to honor that and respect where he was, which was a different place than me, and accept that sometimes you can absolutely love someone completely, and still not be with them.

For his birthday, I recorded a poem I wrote for him which detailed all of the emotions he brought out in me, both the good and the not so good. When he wrote me back, I once again remembered what I admired so much about him.

"I'm grateful for you," he wrote. "I'm grateful for everything we experienced together, and every seed we planted in one another. I'm sorry for pain that was caused in the process, it was never my intention to hurt you in any way. But I am happy for the love that was cultivated from us taking a chance and following our instincts. I love you and appreciate you baring your soul with such a beautiful piece."

I smiled at my phone and a few tears found their way down my cheeks.

I wrote back, "I reckon it's never one's intention to hurt the people they truly love, but it happens sometimes. There was always a part of me that thought throughout all these years that if we ever had a chance to explore what was there between us, it'd be magical and it'd be the one that stuck. At least one of those things is true. I love you more than you will ever know, and every moment with you is a memory I will cherish until the next life. I hope you had an amazing birthday and that you were showered with the light that you bring to so many people's lives. Thank you for being so godly, and for helping me see the god in me. I'm so proud of the man you are and the man you're becoming."

You'd think the story ended there, and in all honesty, I kinda wish it did. This was the perfect opportunity to practice what I'd been preaching and let everything move forward gracefully, even though it wasn't the way I'd hoped. But nope. Every time I was teased with the chance to cling back on, I did, therefore proving to myself that there were still some lessons I was too stubborn to accept.

Even after weeks of not speaking, we'd always find our way back to one another, and it would seem as though nothing would miss a beat. We'd catch up on everything we missed, and I'd try to casually ask about his love life (although, I'm sure he saw right through it). He always told me there was nothing going on, and I'd be lying if I said I wasn't happy to hear that.

However, if you know anything about a woman's intuition, you know that it's one of our most sacred gifts.

My intuition kept telling me that although we were spending time together again, although there was still a sense of love there, there was also another woman in the picture. Instead of assuming, I went back to our very first conversation and the vow that we made, and simply asked him about it. He said there was nothing going on.

I wasn't completely convinced, but what could I do? He wasn't my boyfriend, anyway. All I could do was hope that he respected our friendship enough to tell me the truth and take whatever he said.

After some more time in this limbo with him, I came to a point where I thought that maybe I should have sex again. And maybe, it should be with him. So, during a conversation at my apartment, I brought it to his attention.

"This is going to sound out of the blue, I'm sure, but I've been feeling like I started this no-sex journey for a reason, and now I'm losing sight of why I need to keep it going. I just feel deprived of affection. I want to have sex, but I want to have it with you, because I trust you. I know that if you choose to do it with me, it'd be for the right reasons, but I want to know how you feel about that."

Looking back, I couldn't tell you for sure if I gave this proposal with genuine intentions. I really felt as though that was the case at the time, but in retrospect, there may have been underlying motives to take this situationship to another level. I guess that unhealthy part of me was still there, despite not getting any for two years.

He was surprised, but a smile crept on his face. "Well," he began. "I think that'd be beautiful. But if there's any piece of you that feels like you'd regret it, then maybe we should rethink it."

"I wouldn't regret it."

"Then, let's do it."

Inside me there was a little, sex-deprived girl both cheering and riddled with anxiety over the fact that she was gonna do it with this guy. But it wasn't going to happen in that moment. Before he left, I half-jokingly said, "So, just let me know when you wanna do it."

He smiled and said, "Oh, I already have an idea."

You know how they say your gut knows things before you do? Yeah, the excitement of that conversation didn't last long before I started feeling sick about it. I wasn't sure if I was just nervous, psyching myself out or if my body was telling me something my mind refused to accept, but I was overwhelmed with the fact that I shouldn't do this. I kept trying to ignore it, though. I kept trying to push the visions I had of him with another woman out of my head, because it was just my insecurities, right? Having sex with him would totally be for the right reasons.

Right?

More time passed, and all of a sudden, I started hearing that he was dating the girl that had my intuition buzzing. I was stunned at the thought that this man, my friend, who loves and cares for me, would agree to doing something he knows means very much to me if he was involved with someone else. So, I asked if he was free to talk to gain some clarity on the situation. He said he needed to deal with some other things before he could talk to me.

Sigh.

I tried to remain patient and calm, but when a week went by with nothing from him, I chose to write out my final goodbye (an act that I'd mastered at this point), including everything that had been mulling in my mind, and send it off along with my sexual fantasies. Days after sending that essay of a text, he contacts me to tell me that we "DEFINITELY need to talk" because there was clearly a misunderstanding. OK, I thought. Maybe I was wrong. Let's talk.

Except whenever I tried to make time for the conversation *he* initiated, I was met with silence. Later that week, while trying to remain calm even though there were a lot of unanswered questions, I went to a party for his family, and my stomach dropped. She was there with him.

Guess there's my answer.

To say that felt like a slap in the face would be an understatement. It wasn't just seeing what I'd hoped would never come true right there in front of my face, but it was the fact that this situation made me feel like I didn't deserve the common decency of a conversation before being bombarded with what was going on. A heads up would've been nice. I felt ambushed.

I faked a smile while my insides felt like they were being suffocated. It's a feeling anyone who's felt betrayed by someone they love knows all too well.

It's not courtesy from a lover that I expected. It was respect from a friend. Regardless of our inconsistency and lack of labels, I truly believed that we both held each other to a high regard, and it was like I couldn't even have the luxury of mourning the death of whatever it was that we had before being met with the gut-wrenching image of seeing a man I loved with another woman.

Later that night, he called me to finally have that conversation that, at that point, was hours too late. He expressed his frustration with everything, explaining that the entire situation was a whirlwind and venting about the difficulty with transparency. I expressed my frustrations and pain with his actions, and we tried to end on civil terms, but I knew before I hung up that nothing was going to be the same after that. The man I thought I knew would *never* have put me through that, but it was time to accept that the man I fell in love with was gone.

Maybe he never even existed.

It was one of those moments where I really had to ask myself, "Was I mad because I felt like he lied about the type of man he was? Or was I mad because I lied to myself about the type of man he was?"

I remained distant, despite his attempts to rekindle our friendship. "I need time to heal," I told him candidly. "OK, I can respect that. Whenever you're ready, I'll be here."

But that wasn't entirely true. He was really only there when it was convenient for him, because the reality of our interaction during our time together was that he always had a hard time following through with anything—from the handful of difficult conversations that were constantly put on pause to pleading to meet my dad, because "it would mean a lot to me," only to never actually do it when my father came to visit. I'd always (maybe foolishly) get my hopes up, only to be disappointed, and I learned that he was more consistent with letting me down than anything else.

The man who told me he loved me, cared for me, respected me, never wanted to hurt me, the man who read about guys who'd betrayed me in the past, the man who chipped away at my walls just to intently listen as I recalled some of my most hurtful memories was now becoming another name on that list.

Regardless of knowing that he just wasn't it and we weren't meant to be a forever thing, it was hard not to take everything that happened personally. I felt stupid. I felt so, so stupid.

I remember thinking; no wonder people close up and never love again. Why would they when *this* can happen?! But once my pity party was over, I remembered—Bruna, loving someone with all of your being is never stupid.

I gave myself permission to love and be loved in return instead of running the moment I got scared. I didn't actively push him away, even though the idea crept to mind. I may have entertained the thought of manipulating the situation when it didn't follow the picture I envisioned in my head, but I didn't go through with it. I didn't succumb to the superficial demands society places on what constitutes as love and a relationship. I learned how to not only grow within myself, but with someone alongside the journey. I revealed all of my innermost flaws and secrets, because I was no longer afraid of whether or not they deemed me worthy. I deemed myself worthy, and when our path to continue together was no longer in sight, my value did not decrease just because his position in my life was swapped with empty space.

And that, my sweet, is not stupid. That's brave.

Sure, I probably prolonged the situation and could work on my boundary issues, but let's focus on the positive.

I honored where he was in his life, and despite the heaviness it created in my chest, I tried to just *go with the flow*, which is unheard of territory for me. I was able to practice the love I preach for myself by bowing out once I realized that I was in a situation that no longer served me in the direction I was trying to go. Lastly, I learned that I didn't need anyone's blessing but my own to fully let go.

None of that is to say it was simple. There were plenty of heavy cries bursting from an anxious heart. There were a lot of nights feeling rejected, replaced and abandoned. There was a lot of anger that I wasn't sure how to channel, because I always thought the healthy way to process anger was to dismiss it, but that does no good for anybody, because then the energy just lingers. I had to honor the anger I felt, but in a way that didn't make me engage in behavior I'd regret once the dust settled. I had to acknowledge my feelings without the need to react. *Aha!* That was the big plot twist.

I was so used to being dramatic and impulsive and creating this big show when my feelings were hurt, because how dare you. But for what? At the end of the day, they're still gonna be going about their life while you're pissed off. The only difference is now they know just how much they affect you, and it's not about denying that, but letting go of the need to include anyone else in your journey to move forward. I kept feeling like we had to have a final bow so that I could move on without all this anger I had in my heart for him, but after agreeing to talk, he went ghost again, and I had to pay attention to the big, glaring neon sign staring me blank in the face:

YOU DON'T NEED ANYONE ELSE'S PERMISSION TO MOVE ON.

I was the only one trying so hard to revive something that begged to die. What was I fighting for? I had to learn to be OK with accepting what is and letting go on my own, because the only way to truly get your power back is to stop revolving your life around the actions (or inactions) of someone else.

When it comes to two people in love, cause and effect are not always correlated the way we'd like to believe. We just convince ourselves that's the case, because drawing linear theories to emotional equations makes us feel safe, but it doesn't always work out that way. Understanding love is not always easy. Recognizing happiness is not always easy. Practicing self-worth and self-care is not always easy—especially when all you've known is the opposite, when all you've allowed yourself is the opposite, when all you kept feeding yourself was the idea that the opposite is all you deserved.

The One Who Tested My Growth

He came into my life, ever so slowly, with so much subtlety that mirrored the mystery of his heart, and created an environment that initially made me feel safe enough to bloom on my own. And perhaps that was all that was meant to come of this all along. I proved to myself that despite all of the heartbreak and unfortunate situations I've endured in the past, I am always able to love again. Despite this heartbreak, I will love again.

I proved to myself that I am able to bare my soul completely and wholly to another man. I am able to show love and affection to another man, and receive it back. I am able to let go without fearing whether I've done too much or not done enough, because I know that I did my best, and my best is always good enough.

I proved to myself that I am the type of woman who can attract men with admirable qualities—men who are kind, pure, intelligent, spiritual and filled with genuine love and care—so there very well may be a man who can offer me everything I valued so much in these relationships and more, because he'll be ready and willing to reciprocate the love and commitment I was ready to invest.

I proved to myself that I always know better, I just don't always listen, and the simple act of listening to myself can save me from so much self-inflicted heartache, sabotage and darkness.

I allowed myself to revel in the celebration that I surrendered to love the best way I knew how. I showed up unapologetically and honestly. I was able to love and receive love as it was happening, and I was able to let go when the love could no longer grow.

That's the beautiful thing about pain. When you're able to step outside of it and see all of the priceless lessons that come from some of the ugliest moments, you begin to find meaning in everything.

When you find meaning, you find acceptance, and when you find acceptance, you can finally feel peace.

And with that, I was able to take all my harbored anger and resentment, and let it go.

8

The One Who Raised Me

Opening my heart means opening all of me and sometimes I'm not happy with what I see.

Will you leave?

Will I leave before I'm left because the fear of another disappointment weighs heavily on me?

See, they tell me to let it go, but he's the only man to ever know the deepest parts of me.

After all, he watched me grow.

My father, who didn't know how to love his daughter, who didn't know how to talk to her father.

Once daddy's little girl, but no more.

Somewhere between adolescence and divorce, the bond was torn and no one cared to fix it anymore.

And when he said he was going to leave, I wanted to beg, 'No, please,' but the guilt said goodbye, and I racked another lie when I told my father I'd be ok if he started a new life.

How can I be mad when I pushed away my dad, but fuck, I was a kid who didn't know what she had.

Now I chase after men as if that will fix me within, trying to fill a void that you were supposed to be in.

And when they decide to leave, I beg, 'No, please,' because I can't take another man turning his back on me.

You make it seem so easy.

Maybe you don't need me.

How can I expect a man to stay when my own father leaves me?

I kept saying it was OK, because I knew you were unhappy

And that's what I always do, put me behind you.

But I needed you here, and I needed to hear that you love me, and you're proud of me, and I'm doing it right.

But I didn't get that, right?

Instead I get yearly calls and some texts, but mainly nothing at all.

The distance keeps us safe from having to face the fact that we've both made mistakes.

You were the first man I've ever loved and no matter how hard I tried, I never felt enough.

ALL I WANTED WAS AN EXAMPLE OF HOW TO BE LOVED BY A MAN, BUT NOW I'M RUNNING IN CIRCLES TRYING TO FIGURE IT OUT AGAIN.

BECAUSE YOU COULDN'T SHOW ME.

YOU COULDN'T GET THIS DEEP.

AND I'M LEFT WITH THIS EMPTY HOPE THAT SOMEDAY, A MAN WILL TRULY LOVE ME.

I guess you could say I was a daddy's girl growing up. My days at school always ended with the excitement of going home to tell him what I'd learned and to show him all the A's I'd get (because God forbid, I got a B). We'd sit together in the den, which was full of his favorite books, pick out something to get lost in, and I'd read to him. He loved history, so that was a common topic, but I just couldn't get into it. Every time he wanted to discuss something from our past, I'd rebuke: "Why are we talking about what already happened?" (Ha, I wish I approached my love life with that kind of mentality.)

"Because Bruna," he'd tell me, "We must remember where we've been to know where we're going."

He would talk my ear off about US history and mainly, Lebanon. He really wanted me to know about the country

I was born in, and where he risked his life to fight for those who lived there.

My dad was the Commander of the Special Defense in the Lebanese Forces with his own base and 300 men under his command. Although he had obvious leadership qualities, he didn't seem like the type of man who shouted orders and ran around deserted terrain with an AK in his hand to those who'd meet him. He was soft-spoken, patient and kind. But the fighter in him did peek through here and there. Along with books, my dad introduced me to the wonderful world of movies. We'd always go on movie dates, and I'll never forget the first time he took me to an actual theater. We went to watch the 1994 Ray Liotta and Whoopi Goldberg film, *Corrina, Corrina* at the local mall, and I was so nervous. I remember looking at him, and asking, "Dad, what if I have to pee during the movie?"

"Well, you get up and go pee and then come back." I didn't realize that was allowed. I was that girl who would sit in my seat at school, and never get up, so I figured this was the same deal, but turns out my bladder was way too invested, and a bathroom run didn't end up being necessary.

Movies became our thing. In fact, after learning that my parents were going to divorce, the first thing I asked my mom was, "Who's going to go to the movies with me now?" My dad and I made sure we'd still go together, usually on Christmas Day when everyone's off doing their jolly festivities. We'd head to the mall and watch a flick. One year, we saw *Munich*, and there was a very brooding scene where Eric Bana's character was lagging on pulling the trigger. So what does my dad do? He yells, "Oh, c'mon, just shoot him!" I gave him a mortified look, and that's when I think he realized he was in a public place, and maybe encouraging someone to shoot someone else wasn't the smartest idea. That's what I mean when I say his war persona would peek through.

However, aside from everything else, his most prevalent and admirable quality was his loyalty. He was fiercely loyal to everything and everyone he loved. So much so, that when he decided to move back to Lebanon, he told me, "Bruna, there are families there who I still feel obligated to protect." While I understood where he was coming from, I can't say it didn't sting.

It's hard to write about my father, because our relationship was rocky. When I was a young girl, I adored him. I'd prance into the room all dressed up just to hear him say *scheeeel*, which is Lebanese slang that basically meant, "Oh dang, girl, look at you." He was like a superhero to me. He always seemed to have the answers to everything, which is why I'd make him buy me those 100-random-question-and-answer books, so I could just sit there and ask him every single one. I was always a curious child, and I think he's the one that sparked that. I remember one day, we were sitting together, and I asked him out of the blue, "Dad, do monkeys eat sandwiches?" And he smiled, and said, "Hm, I don't know. That's a good question." I felt like I won the lottery. It's silly to think that an off-the-cuff question like that is what really fueled who I am today, but there's some validity there. The feeling I felt when he said that I asked a good question was a feeling I never wanted to lose. So I continued to ask good questions, and I still ask a million questions to this day. Perhaps that's why I became a journalist (slash over-thinker)? Either way, my intrigue for questioning everything around me, and everything about myself, instead of accepting what I see for face value, is what has helped me become someone who is always thirsty for knowledge. I love that about myself, and I got that from him.

Things took a shift once I entered my teens, which might not sound surprising because adolescence is basically Hell on Earth, both for the person going through it and everyone around them. However, my experience was heightened because of my parents' decision to split.

It was Thanksgiving night in 2000. I was a soon-to-be 13-year-old, getting dressed up for the holiday for the first time because we were never big on going all out for these occasions. In our old, one-bedroom apartment, my mom would put up a fake 3-foot tree with some lights and some garland for Christmas, and Thanksgiving wasn't even really a thing. But this year was different.

We were finally able to move into a house, which meant I finally had my own room, and we had a fireplace, which has always been my favorite thing. My mom, who is an amazing cook, made us a feast, and it was the first time that we really had Thanksgiving as a family. After dinner, we went into the living room, and my parents said they had to tell me something. And that's when they dropped the bomb on me, "We're getting a divorce."

Did I just become Chandler from *Friends*?

To be honest, I don't remember my reaction. Maybe because it didn't sink in? Maybe because I saw it coming? Maybe because I was still in a turkey coma and wondering why the fuck they would tell me this now? Regardless, it was happening, and when I told my best friend at school that week, she laughed and thought I was pulling another prank. It wasn't until I started to cry that she pulled me in and held me. It was the first time I'd ever cried in front of anybody like that.

Every one of my friends were shocked to hear about what was happening, because every time they came over, things seemed fine. My parents weren't overly affectionate, but they weren't cold, either. Once the news was out, though, they stopped pretending. My mom moved her stuff into the den and made that her new bedroom. The fights weren't behind closed doors anymore, and I was just in the midst of it all—a 13-year-old only child trying to figure out what the fuck was happening while also feeling like I had no outlet or direction on how to deal with something like this. I didn't really have people I could talk to about it. All of my friends at the time had that perfect, cookie-cutter family, or at least it looked that way, with the house, and the dog and the clothes from Nordstrom. I never felt like I fit into their world. I ate "weird" pita sandwiches, wore clothes from the sale bin at TJ Maxx, and was never allowed to eat fast food. I was raised by a family who was very frugal, and at the time, I was embarrassed of it, because I was an ungrateful brat who just wanted to be like all the cool kids. But now, well, now I realize I owe everything to my parents for trying to make my life continue seamlessly as best they could, even though everything was turned upside-down. This was new territory for all of us.

As you can imagine, money became even tighter when my mom moved out and took me with her. We'd have to go to custody hearings and those just always brought out the ugly side of everyone. My mom was stressed to the point that she wondered why she was still alive. My dad was angry and became spiteful. And I was just...there. The middleman trying to deflect the negative energy coming at me from every angle, but at such a young age, it felt nearly impossible.

The routine never got easier. For five years, I'd pack my bag on Fridays, go to my dad's after school, spend the weekend with him (meaning, I ate Chef Boyardee for dinner every night and then tried to leave the house every chance I got), and then return to my mom's on Sunday— but not before having uncomfortable chats with Dad.

He always tried to sway my desire to spend most of my time at mom's, constantly trying to persuade me to live with him instead. I wish I could say it was to have me around more, but I don't know if that's true. It could've been because he was outraged at how much child support was. So, before I left every Sunday, we'd sit in the living room and he would talk to me about things I didn't care to talk about, like what he thought about my mother, her past, things that went on during their marriage, while I just held back tears. I resented him for that.

No, Dad, telling me shit about Mom isn't going to make me want to live with you. You had better luck buying me that canopy bed set from Burlington.

I spent a lot of time alone, because my mom was working so much to make ends meet. Even though I didn't mind time to myself, they became worrisome, because that also became the time that my Dad would sporadically stop by, banging on the door and yelling for me. I'd be doing homework and then go hide. I didn't want him to see me. I didn't want to open the door. I was afraid he was going to force me to leave with him, because what my parents didn't know was that I came across an email he wrote to my Mom when the browser was still open on the computer, and he threatened to take me to Lebanon with him and said she'd never see me again. That led to my mom getting a restraining order. Unless I was at his house during the court ordered days, he wasn't allowed to come near us, and to this day, whenever I hear loud banging on the door or window, a part of me wants to crawl under the bed and just close my eyes until it stops.

It was all beginning to be too much. I didn't act out as much as you'd think I would, but I definitely tried to escape. I hung out with the wrong crowd. I'd sneak out of my Dad's place in the middle of the night to meet up with friends or the awful guy I was dating. I just didn't want to be in the suffocating bubble that I felt I was in. I did write, though. That was always my release. But one day, what came from my fingertips wasn't something any parent would want to read.

I kept blaming myself for their divorce. What could I have possibly done, you ask? Nothing, really, but there was instantly a part of me that felt like my family was broken because of me. Layer that guilt with the mounting pressure and anger coming at me from both sides, and I just didn't want to do it anymore. So, I decided to write a poem about suicide. I wrote that maybe the world would be a better place if I wasn't in it anymore, because everyone around me was so unhappy. I tore it out of my journal, and I placed it on my mom's bed. After she read it, she ripped it to shreds and said, "Don't ever write shit like this again."

Maybe not the best response, sure. But I couldn't even imagine what went through her mind. That's not something a mother wants to read from her only child.

I never wrote shit like that again. But the thought of suicide, well the thought lingered for a while. I never did it, clearly. I never even really attempted it. It was scary enough to know that my mind could go there so fast.

Once I turned 18, I was legally dismissed from having to go to my Dad's house every weekend, but I felt like it wasn't right to just ditch him. I may not have been able to say, "I love you, too," on the phone to him, but he was still my Dad, and I was all he had. Just as things began to simmer in our relationship, tension was rising in Lebanon. In 2006, the rise of Hezbollah, a Shi'a Islamist militant group, sparked a war in our country that ultimately led to the death of roughly 1,300 Lebanese civilians. One of them being my grandfather.

I mentioned a lot of things my Dad is, but something he is not is emotional, which lent its fair share of problems between us. But we'll get there.

The first, and last, time I ever heard my Dad cry was when I was 19 years old and getting ready for bed. He called my cell phone and asked what I was doing that Sunday. I said "nothing," and through tears, he asked me, "Will you go with me to my father's memorial service?"

My heart broke. It didn't break because my grandfather died, which I know sounds extremely cold-hearted, but the truth of the matter is I don't know my family that well. I traveled to America with my parents when I was a year old, and it was always just the three of us. My heart broke because my father's father died, a man I knew he always looked up to, a man my mother always spoke fondly of, a man who my dad hadn't seen in 19 years because of me, and now he'd never see him again. The guilt was almost overwhelming at this point. Choked up, I told him of course I'd be there, and so I went to church with him and our family friends, a mix of men he'd fought in the army with and their wives. We all went to Wahib's, a popular Lebanese restaurant in Alhambra, Calif., for a traditional feast, and in between stuffing our face with delicious food, my dad would reminisce on old memories with his buddies, while I'd sit across women who would ask me if I remembered that they once changed my diaper. I managed to stop the impulse of responding with, "Is that a serious question?" and just smiled instead.

After my grandfather's death, my dad said he had to go visit his mom and siblings in Lebanon. Just to give you an idea, my dad's side of the family is huge. He was one of nine children, and most of them had about five kids each (because that's how Middle Easterners do it... except for my family, of course). I couldn't even tell you how many cousins I have and I know for a fact I haven't met all of them to this day. The night before he left to Lebanon to visit, I typed a letter and left it out for him. I apologized for being so cold to him for so many years, and for blaming him for a lot of things that I didn't like in my life. I told him I love you for the first time in a really long time, and it wasn't because I felt guilty or sad for his loss. It was because in that moment, I remembered the Dad I grew up loving so much, and he was about to leave to a dangerous country, and there's something very frightening about saying goodbye to someone who you feel you may never see again. So, I spoke my peace through my fingers, as I always do, and off he went.

Slowly, but surely, our relationship began to mend, but his back and forth to Lebanon to watch over his family after my grandfather's death became quite expensive, especially since an accident years prior left him unable to work. That's when he came to the decision that he should just move back. He'd always wanted to return to Lebanon at some point, and when he came to me for my blessing, how could I say no? At that point, he devoted 20 years of his life for me, away from everything and everyone he knew, and the guilt I felt for everything that happened between us up until that point made me feel like keeping him from moving back to where he felt at home was incredibly selfish. So, I said OK. He packed up all of his things, and just like that, he was gone.

We tried to keep in constant contact, but that didn't last long. The truth is we have a better relationship when we give each other some space. I went to visit not too long after he left, and he seemed happy with his brothers and sisters. He was always surrounded by people who love and care for him, and when my grandmother passed away, I knew he was grateful that he was able to cherish the extra years he got with her.

He flew back a year later for my college graduation, which ended up being a wash because he sat at the wrong ceremony. "Bruna, why didn't I hear your name?" Um, because you were sitting at the Business commencement, Dad. He was pissed, rightfully so. I was pissed, because I was always pissed about something. Plus, tensions were high because it was the first time he met my stepdad. Yeah, awkward doesn't even begin to cover it. My dad refused to go to the graduation party my mom and Dave set up for me, so instead, we went to our usual spot for dinner—North Woods Inn.

As I sat across from him, drooling over the cheese bread and salads that they're famous for, I felt like a very accomplished young woman. At 23 years old, I had my Bachelor's Degree in Communications, and a full-time job with a pretty nifty salary waiting for me at a company I'd always dreamed of working for. Of course, that's not what he saw. He wasn't too impressed with my job as an Entertainment News Writer. "When are you going to let go of that teenage fantasy, Bruna?" He always wanted me to be a lawyer or a doctor or a "real" journalist covering hard news and global conflict.

And if it wasn't the job that was the issue, it was my lifestyle.

"When are you going to get married and have kids?"

Jesus-fucking-Christ Dad, I just graduated college, can I live for a second, please?

I worked my ass off for as long as I could remember. I was the first one to go to college, I juggled 21 units at two colleges simultaneously, worked an internship and a job, and although I am inherently one who enjoys challenges and working myself to the bone, I know that deep down, a lot of the accomplishments I gained never seemed as grand as they were, because I never got the praise I was looking for from him. My dad told me he was proud of me once, and it wasn't verbal, it was written in my graduation card. It was one of the very few times that he didn't just sign the card and let the pre-written message speak for him, and I cried seeing those words scribbled down in his writing.

See, it took me a very long time to recognize what affect this all had on me. Throughout my troubling attempts at love with various men, I knew, from the bare bones of Psychology I learned that any therapist would begin to find the root of the problem by tracing it back to my relationship with my father. But every time I'd try to analyze it myself, I came up empty-handed. Sure, we had our problems, but that's normal. He never hit me, he didn't abuse me in any way, he didn't run out on us. It wasn't until many years later that I began to see what I was blind to before, and it hit me all at once like a dump truck.

While writing a letter to my younger self for my website The Problem With Dating, I touched on the fact that I never really got the satisfaction of making my father proud. This became a topic of conversation with my stepdad, who would often read what I posted and then spark a discussion about it with me afterwards. I was visiting him and my mom one Sunday, when we began to talk about my relationship with my father. Dave never really brought him up, because he never wanted to overstep his boundaries, and I respected him for that. But when he said, "I just can't imagine leaving my daughter," something inside me broke.

My initial response was defensive, because even though he had innocent intentions, that's my dad you're talking about. "Well, it's not like we got along that well. What was he supposed to do?"

"Yeah, nobody got along with their parents at 19," he argued. And he made a good point.

I don't know what it was, but I had to excuse myself from the table and proceeded to lock myself in the bathroom while I sobbed. For the first time, maybe ever, I realized that my Dad's decision to leave had a greater impact than I was willing to admit. I kept making excuses about why it was OK, but that's when the common theme began to play out—every man I loved, left, and instead of letting them go, I'd hold on tighter and try to prove my worth to them so that they would stay. So maybe, just maybe, I wasn't doing that for them, but I was doing that for me. I was doing that for the young girl who said goodbye to her father with secret hopes that he'd change his mind and stay, because I'm worth staying for, right? Whether it was compassion or pride that stopped me from saying, "No, Dad, I need you here with me. I don't care if we had a rough past, a girl needs her father around," the consequences hit me the same.

I just wanted a man to show me that I'm worth staying for, because it's awful to feel like you're so easy to leave. For that reason, I kept going above and beyond for every man that crossed my path, and because I wanted the praise and validation to fill the void that my father left me with.

This realization took roughly 10 years to understand, and when it happened, it was all so fast. It's like I was finally in on the joke everyone knew for years, and to this day, speaking about this makes me break down in tears. The first time I said any of this out loud was during a spontaneous dinner with one of my best friends at Cheesecake Factory. I explained the revelation to her over our pasta and bread, and the tears came flowing out. She asked if I planned to talk to my dad about this, to confront him with how I felt. I said no. Although a part of me felt like maybe it should happen, another part of me felt like it wasn't necessary, because despite all of this, I wasn't angry at him.

The crazy thing is the older I get, the less I look at my parents as my parents, and more as people. This was a man, who went through a 20-year war, was taken hostage and escaped, has stories that he refuses to share with me out of protection, left the only place he knew as home and created a life for a little human. He probably didn't know the first thing about being a parent, but he did the best he could. He, as a man with his own demons and past, did the best he could. And I can't fault him for making mistakes along the way. Especially when some of those faults helped create some of my strongest qualities. Anybody who knows me knows I'm a hard worker, and perhaps that's partially due to his high standard. Anybody who knows me knows I'm emotional and overwhelm those close to me with love, and perhaps that's because I craved it so much from him. I fought to become the woman I am today, and when it comes to being a fighter for everything I love, it's easy to see who I got that from.

I'm not angry because now I'm aware, and the self-awareness provides me with the tools to move forward from whatever was holding me back before, and that's something I've been trying to grasp for a very long time.

However, even with this realization, I later came to understand that there was still a lot of fixing that needed to take place, and it would never get better without saying the things that had been left unsaid. As you know, I always pride myself on being the type of person who lays it all out on the table. I don't expect you to read my mind, because I state it and let you take the lead on how you want to handle it, but for whatever reason, I would act differently with my father.

So here I was, thousands of miles away from him, and expecting him to *just know* that I had deep-rooted pain from our tumultuous relationship that was still weighing me down in my late 20s. So, I did something about it.

During a random WhatsApp text conversation with my Dad, I asked him, "Are you proud of me?"

"I am just thinking why you're asking me this question," he responded. I was instantly annoyed at what seemed to me as another attempt to deflect.

"Because I want to know the answer," I simply stated.

"I am proud of you no matter what. Even though sometimes you hurt me."

My instinct was to get defensive, to respond in shouty capitals with, "WHAT THE HELL DO YOU MEAN HURT YOU? YOU HURT ME!" But I knew better, and for a man who was always so stoic and repressive of showing any emotion, I needed to take this opportunity to put my ego aside, and maximize his touch of vulnerability with some compassion.

So I asked, "How do I hurt you?"

He told me, "You blame me for things that happened in your life."

I let that simmer for a moment as I contemplated the best way to respond.

"I have [blamed you for things that happened in my life]. And sometimes I still do, but then again, I'm older now. I'm able to see you as a man instead of my father who I looked up to as some superhero. Dad, you have to understand that growing up you were the most important man to me and all those years when we couldn't even be in the same room together without there being tension broke my heart. And I was mad and I acted like I didn't need you and that you leaving didn't matter but it did and I'm sorry. I love you, I always have and I always will, and there is no denying that you and I are very different but we're also so much alike. I am your daughter, I'm reminded of that every day. My love of books and movies I get from you. My patience and loyalty, I get from you. My eagerness to learn, I get from you. I love those things about me. And now that I can separate you from the ideal I had in my head to just a man, I can empathize."

I continued, "You went through things I will never even know, and you did your best given the circumstances. Maybe you regret some things, I know I do, but we both made mistakes, and I forgive you for whatever happened. I just needed to hear that you're proud of me and that you love me and that I'm not fucking everything up because you never really tell me and I need to hear that from you. You're my father. I'll always need you."

After expressing that there are many things that require a face-to-face conversation, he said, "You know I love you dearly, you are the only person left in this world that I care for the most. We may have differences, of course, but you will always be my little angel. Just keep in mind what makes you happy makes me happy and what hurts you hurts me, too. You are in my heart always. I love you, too, and I'm proud of you, never forget that."

Everything I had longed to hear for so many years, words left unsaid that stirred up so much resentment, finally brought some peace into my life. And all I had to do was have the courage to initiate a difficult conversation that, after the fact, wasn't all that difficult at all.

After that conversation, he made more effort into checking in, which I appreciated, and I decided that a visit is long overdue.

One of my best friends, who is also Lebanese, was getting married, and I needed a date. I figured, this is perfect. I'll throw it out there to see if he'd want to go with me. He'll be in his element, so it won't be super weird, and, as my life coach astutely observed, I was fearful that he wouldn't make the trip just to see me, so the wedding served as a great cover.

I asked my father if he'd be my date to the wedding, he said OK, and after about a week or two, he booked his flight.

This was really happening.

The second his trip was confirmed, my anxiety went through the roof. At this point in time, my dad and I hadn't seen each other in seven years, and hadn't spent a significant amount of time together under one roof in over 13 years. And now, he was about to stay with me at my apartment for five weeks. As someone who relishes in her solitude, having anyone in my space for that long is huge, let alone my father who I have a topsy-turvy relationship with.

I was feeling both excited and nervous as hell as the countdown to his arrival got smaller and smaller. What would we do? What if he hates it here? What if we fight the whole time? What if I get frustrated and have nowhere to go? What if he disapproves of my lifestyle and judges me for not being where he wants me to be in life?

So many questions that did absolutely no good, because they were all based on "what if?" I quickly realized that was a rabbit hole into depressing territory, so I shifted my focus into what I knew.

I knew that I'm a different person now than who I was the last time we saw each other. I'm grown, and in addition to my own personal development, I was also in training to be a life coach for high conscious living, so I was literally equipped with the tools to deal with whatever situation arose the best way I knew how. I made a list of possible activities and places to go, in case we ever found ourselves with nothing to do, and I reminded myself that regardless of what he says about my lifestyle (being single with no kids and working from home as a freelancer, which has zero stability), *I* was happier than I'd ever been, and that's what matters the most, because while his praise is appreciated, it's not necessary to validate my worth.

I had enlisted my best friend to go with me to the airport and video record our reunion. I wanted to document that experience for the future, because I knew that no matter what happened during his visit, those moments were going to be the most genuine and pure and I didn't want to forget it. While waiting at LAX, and scrambling from one gate to another because of last minute changes, my stomach was in knots and I couldn't contain my emotions. I would burst into tears in the most random moments. I stood front and center among numerous other people who were anxiously awaiting a reunion with a loved one, hoping that my Dad wouldn't miss me in the crowd.

After years of waiting for this moment, I saw him and his bright white hair come out and look for me. I kept yelling, "Dad," and he followed my voice until he finally saw me. We hugged, and I burst into tears like a little girl. Once he let go, he looked down at my face, still crying, and gave me a look that was everything I ever needed to see from him.

"I know," he softly said, and pulled me back in for another hug.

"Who's that," he then whispered in my ear. I forgot my friend was there recording everything. I laughed, and introduced them. We started walking back to my car and it was still very surreal for both of us to be next to each other. "I can't believe this is happening, it feels like a dream," he said. "I am my happiest right now."

Look at him expressing emotion! Guess I wasn't the only one who changed. Time will do that to you.

However, it took *maybe* 30 minutes before we quickly spiraled into the conversations that I was dreading. "So what are you doing for work? Why aren't you married? Bruna, I want grandkids. Do you go to church? Jesus died for your sins..."

Breathe, Bruna. Breathe.

I tried to maintain my composure, and if I felt like I was going to get snappy, I'd just take deep breaths. When we finally got back to my apartment, he seemed very pleased. *Phew!* It was already late, so I let him know that my room was his and to get some rest.

"No, no, no. I'm going to sleep on the couch," he told me. "I don't want to intrude. Just go about your life as you normally would."

It was a sweet sentiment, but an unrealistic one. Nothing would be normal for those five weeks. I barely worked, because that meant time away from my father, and in all honesty, my energy was all over the place. I didn't feel like myself, which I suppose is completely understandable, because I was thrown into different territory.

There were definitely moments during his visit that tested my patience. Whether it was small things like chores around the apartment or bigger things like his assumptions on what my life *should* be like, I'd find myself running to my best friend's house for some space, because sometimes, even the deepest of breaths wouldn't have helped.

"You're a freelancer, right?"

"Yes, Dad."

"Well, since you're not doing anything, you should just move back to Lebanon."

Sigh. Don't get mad, Bruna. His generation doesn't understand this line of work. He doesn't mean it the way it sounds.

Still, I knew that would be the case, and the good times outweighed all of that, anyway.

We binge watched all of *Game of Thrones* together, drinking wine, bonding over our mutual admiration for Ned Stark and laughing over my Dad's incorrect usage of the show's terms.

"They have all the dragon glasses now. They should try to turn the White Waters into humans again."

Oh, is that right? Ha. We died over that one.

More importantly, his time here provided a lot of clarity. He told me stories he'd never shared with me before about his past, his time in the war and how he feels about me and the divorce. As I mentioned, my dad was never an emotionally expressive person, and the void of seeing that emotion for a long time translated to me as a lack of love in our relationship. But that wasn't the case at all.

I caught a glimpse of my photo as the wallpaper on his phone, I saw photos of me as a little girl and a teenager in his wallet, I experienced plenty of moments that proved how much he cared for me, even if it wasn't outwardly expressed in an obvious manner.

During one conversation, he told me that my mother asked him if he ever regretted getting married to her. "How could I? Because if I regret getting married to her," he explained, "then, I, in turn, regret having you. And I would never regret that."

He continued, "I saw so many people die right in front of me. Every time, I thought, I'm next. But that never happened, and I couldn't understand why. Why not me? And then I figured, it must have been so that I could have you."

Of course I cried. It was such a powerful statement.

One night, my dad asked that I invite my best friend out to dinner. We went to North Woods, of course, and the two of them carried the conversation. She became my biggest cheerleader, gushing about me and the type of person I am to him. And then he said something to her that struck me.

"You know, I'd think about reaching out and talking to Bruna all the time, but I figured I'd just be intruding in her life, so I wouldn't."

I sat back, staring into the distance of dim lighting and peanut shells on the floor, and thought, "I wouldn't mind if you intruded."

That's when I realized that all those years, he stopped himself from reaching out because he thought I didn't want him to, while I thought he just didn't care enough about me to check in. One event created two completely different interpretations, and neither one of them were true.

There were a lot of moments like that—moments that forced me to break away from the story I'd created about our relationship, his love (or lack thereof) for me and my worth.

Alcohol also helped bring down the walls a little.

One night, my dad came back from visiting one of his longtime friends, and I don't know for sure, but I *think* he was a little drunk. He was definitely chatty, and that was the first time we had an actual conversation about my love life that didn't include him just judging the fact that I wasn't popping out my third kid by now.

"I've loved many men, Dad. And they'd always act as if they loved me back, and then all of a sudden, they leave," I told him.

"It's not easy for some men to love a strong woman," he responded. "Especially when they know you'd be OK without them."

"Yeah, I guess. But I'm not going to compromise who I am for that. I'm confident that there's a guy who will be thankful I am the way I am, and he'll be the right guy for me."

"Absolutely," he said. "And he'll be very lucky to find a woman like you."

A drunk man's words are a sober man's thoughts, right? I was happy to hear that.

Meanwhile, on the night of the wedding, I decided to let loose—I ended up having six chilled shots of vodka (who am I?). I wasn't *drunk*, but I was just the right amount of tipsy that I got a little ballsy. See, of course I loved my father, and I knew now more than ever that he loved me, too, but when it came to open acts of affection, that was still a little difficult for both of us. Regardless, the Belvedere assisted me in making the first move a couple of times by asking my father to dance.

While slow dancing together, he told me, "I'm so happy I was able to make it out here for this. Thank you. This means a lot to me."

My eyes welled up, and I just pulled closer and let my head rest on his chest.

There was only a short time left at this point before he was going to head back to Lebanon, and I'd always wanted to read and have a picnic at the park with a man I love, so I decided my father (who's also an avid reader) would be the best person to do that with. We went back to my hometown, and munched on some sandwiches while talking about whatever topics came up before diving into our books. At one point, he asked, "What makes you happy?"

"A lot of things. That feeling I get when the sun hits my skin, a calm breeze, good food, a great book, the way the sun lights up my entire apartment around 4 p.m., Jaxon (my cat), my friends, my alone time..."

"Wow," he said. "There are so many different things that make you happy. That's good."

We went on to different things after that, but while walking back to my car, he broke the silence by telling me, "Being here with you. That's what makes me happy."

I smiled. "Thanks, Dad."

When it came time to finally say goodbye again, I remembered how difficult they can be. Sure, I was ready to have my apartment to myself again and to be able to go about my day without having to take anyone else into consideration, but it's so hard to say bye to someone when you don't know when the next hello is going to be.

I pulled the car over at his terminal, helped with the luggage, and while hugging him goodbye, broke into tears. Once he realized what was happening, he held me and said, "Oh, no. Please, Bruna. I won't be able to leave."

We said I love you to each other, one of the few times we'd ever said it in person, and that was that.

When I shared the bare bones of my reunion with my Dad on social media, I received an outpouring of love and many stories from people who were in a similar situation with their fathers. I also got a lot of questions asking why we'd gone so long without seeing each other. I couldn't really tell you. As I explained, we didn't have the best of relationships, and we both saw that in different ways, which allowed us to conveniently use time, money or just "life" as an excuse to not put in the effort to salvage and repair whatever was going on with us.

You don't have to fix what you refuse to acknowledge is broken.

Interpretation was the biggest kryptonite of our relationship, which is also common in many rocky relationships. Something would happen, and instead of talking about it and sharing our feelings or perspective on what we drew from the experience, we comfortably sat in our assumptions and presumed that it was true for the other person, too.

I remember during lunch once, my dad looked at me and said, "You don't need me."

I was shocked at that. "Why would you say that?"

"Because for the last seven years you've been doing just fine."

"Did I have a choice?"

Already there is a lot of open areas for misinterpretation there. What did he constitute as me needing him? How does he define "fine"? What were we each really saying here?

I'll tell you.

As a woman, it's taken me a long time to try and understand a man's point of view on things for obvious reasons (it's not natural for me). But in this situation, my father, and many men for that matter, constitute "being there" for their loved ones as being *financially* there, and that makes sense. Since what feels like the dawn of time, society has drilled it into men that their purpose is to provide stability and security for their family, which is often geared towards financial stability and security.

Meanwhile, I'm over here thinking, of course I need you and I always needed you, *emotionally*. I praise and admire any and every man who goes above and beyond to provide for their family, because I can only imagine how difficult that is, especially with the pressure that's placed from the world, but that's not the be all, end all.

Yeah, I might've been able to make it work with rent and bills and all that, but nothing and no one would have ever been able to take the place of my father's love and his emotional imprint on my life. And that's free.

We want to feel love from our fathers, not just when we're young, but at any age. We want to feel accepted and valued.

Fathers, you are the first man your daughter loves, and the first male role model for your son. Hug them, kiss them, spend time with them, never stop telling them how much they meant to you, even when they roll their eyes and try to push you away. Show them what unconditional love looks like so they can practice it and become it, otherwise they may very well end up chasing fraudulent love disguised as truth because they don't know what the real thing is like.

Show them what it looks like when a man not only uses his logic, resources and intellect, but also his entire heart and emotional depth, because we need those men now more than ever.

And with that, I was able to let my misconstrued relationship with my father go, so that I could enjoy the actual love that was always there.

9

The One Who Saved Me

I looked in the mirror to say goodbye

But first I stared her blank in the eye

I said, "Hey pretty girl, I know it's been rough

And I know there were times when you didn't
feel enough

And I know there were moments when you
wanted to quit

Just end it all while yelling 'fuck this'

But something inside you refused to believe

That anything would be better if you chose to
leave

You started to wonder—maybe you're the
solution

To help revive this superficial institution

"So you showcased your pain for the world to
see

And reminded people about love &
transparency

VULNERABILITY WAS A LOST ART 'TIL YOU MADE IT
YOUR MISSION

AND NOW WHEN YOU TALK, PEOPLE LISTEN

"I KNOW I HAVEN'T MADE IT EASY

AND I KNOW YOU FELT LIKE YOU COULD NEVER PLEASE
ME

I WAS YOUR WORST CRITIC, ALWAYS PUTTING YOU
DOWN

I DIDN'T KNOW ANY BETTER, AND I'M SORRY FOR IT
NOW

WHEN YOU NEEDED ME MOST, I DIDN'T HAVE YOUR
BACK

INSTEAD I WAS BUSY PREPARING MY NEXT ATTACK

I SHOT DOWN EVERYTHING BEAUTIFUL ABOUT YOU

UNTIL IT BECAME NEARLY IMPOSSIBLE FOR YOU TO
LOVE YOU

BUT LUCKILY, YOU WERE STRONGER THAN I KNEW

AND YOU OVERCAME EVERYTHING I PUT YOU THROUGH

YOU'RE BETTER FOR IT, AND IT'S A SIGHT TO SEE

THE FRAGILE GIRL GROW INTO THE WOMAN BEFORE
ME

SHE'S STRENGTH AND GRACE AND EVERYTHING IN
BETWEEN

SHE'S EVERYTHING I NEVER KNEW YOU COULD BE

"AND WHILE I WISH I COULD KEEP YOU CLOSE TO ME

THIS NEXT CHAPTER IS ONE ONLY I CAN SEE

IT'S BITTERSWEET TO MOURN THE GIRL IN FRONT OF
ME

BECAUSE I LOVE YOU, BUT IT'S TIME TO SET YOU FREE

THANK YOU FOR GOING THROUGH HELL AND BACK FOR
ME

WITHOUT YOU, I DON'T KNOW WHERE I'D BE."

Like many young girls, I watched endless Disney films growing up and pictured myself as the princesses. I related to Belle in *Beauty and the Beast* because of her love for books, and to Jasmine in *Aladdin* because she was Middle Eastern (and, if we're gonna keep it *really* real, because she fell for a guy who "wasn't on her level," which ultimately became my aesthetic). But the Disney princess I resonated with the most was Mulan, because for the first time I saw a young girl who didn't wait for Prince Charming to swoop in and save the day. She did that on her own. So, in this chapter, I'm not going to tell you about a guy who rode in, and gave me that magical kiss to mend my heart and make me believe in true love, because there's no guy who could do that for me. This chapter is all about making the decision to save myself.

After my parents' divorce, my mother drilled into my 14-year-old brain that independence was of the utmost importance. "Don't depend on anyone," she'd tell me. Being my mother, and my role model, I took everything she said as gold, and cherished it. I made sure to become the most independent woman you could imagine. I worked two jobs in high school, paid my own bills when necessary, paid for most of my college tuition so I didn't have to take out student loans, got my own place...you get the picture. I was as self-sufficient as they come, and I was so blinded with pride that I neglected to notice the negative impact that bravado could ultimately leave on me.

See, life is all about balance, and while I was pretty good at juggling school or career with my social life, I wasn't so good at creating a peaceful medium with my traits and emotions. I was a very black and white person, so with my heightened independence came the misconstrued notion that vulnerability was a sign of weakness. I always made sure people knew I could handle whatever life threw at me on my own. "I got it," I'd always tell people when they'd offer help.

In turn, love was a one-way street for me. I'd always give it, but never really felt it being returned to me, and it took me a while to realize that it was because I wasn't allowing it to enter my life, even in the subtlest of ways. I'm a great friend, and I can say that with confidence. Those closest to me know that no matter what is going on, they can count on me, but they were resentful that I refused to let them do the same for me. It took me nearly 30 years to feel OK with asking the people who love me most for help without feeling like I was a burden.

When I was younger, I'd fall into that prideful "I don't need you" mentality with boyfriends, because I was taught by society and otherwise that I should never show all my cards, as if the man who is investing a part of his life with me is bound to screw me over. But who wants to be with someone like that? Everyone wants to feel needed. Everyone wants to feel as though they're adding something substantial to the other person's life, and little by little, I started to realize that my steadfast approach to independence was crippling my ability to be a multidimensional woman. Feminine energy is rooted in being graceful and soft, in acknowledging our emotions and being expressive, and I needed to remind myself how to be that way, not just for myself, but for the relationships I cared to cultivate. I knew that to experience healthy love, I needed to not only be completely open to it, but also make sure I was good myself so that I would attract the right type of person. And that would require some major self-work.

I always thought of my brain as this beautiful masterpiece. It'd come up with intriguing questions, it was quick to understand and comprehend complex topics, it was charming and witty, and yet, at some point, it began to work against me. Whether it was the whispers of my past lovers or my ego fueling me with self-doubt, I began to hear so much negativity in relation to who I was as a human being, and I made the mistake of listening.

For years, no one could understand why I would tolerate such unacceptable behavior in my life, or why I constantly thought so lowly of myself. "Why don't you see what we see," my friends would ask me, and it felt like a punch in the gut. Why couldn't I see what they see? The outside world saw a young, attractive, smart, funny, compassionate and driven woman. No one knew of the demons I was fighting behind closed doors. When the world grew silent, and the only company I'd keep were the voices in my head, all I saw was a woman struggling to feel worthy. I wanted to be loved, not realizing that the only love I needed was the love I refused to give myself.

It wasn't difficult to see the patterns in my life. I invested in people who weren't willing to invest the same energy in me, and when they left, I'd beg them to come back by trying to prove myself. When they refused, I'd play the blame game and nestle comfortably in my victim mentality. My friends would feed into that mentality, offering me various solutions on why it didn't work. "He just couldn't handle you," or "You're too good for him, anyway," were quickly shot to my aid. Bless their hearts, they were just trying to help. But that didn't help when it came to confronting the truth—I placed my value in such reckless hands, because I refused to care for it on my own.

I was attracting broken people, because I was broken myself, and the Universe wasn't going to stop giving me these tests until I finally learned my lesson. So how much longer was I going to allow this to happen? Being a master of rhetorical questions, I decided to turn to my hobby of writing as an external passage into my mind. After all, I always say I never know what I'm thinking until I read what I say.

So, when I was 25 years old, I decided to start a fun blog called The Problem With Dating. It was mainly an online journal for myself, documenting shitty dates I'd been on, the constant WTFs of the single life, and practicing my ability to tap into my vulnerability through my safety net of writing. What I didn't expect was for it to become a known platform that resonated with thousands of strangers, who would ultimately witness my journey of self-reflection and self-love that I didn't even know I needed to be on. I was growing in front of people's eyes, and that continues to be the case.

It's strange, because after my 28th birthday, I felt like I was given a new pair of lenses. I saw the world and myself differently, and suddenly, concepts and themes in my personal life that completely puzzled me before seemed clear as day. When I reached out to a girlfriend of mine to express this interesting shift in my life, she simply responded, "Sounds about right. You're in your Saturn Return." Now, I dabble in astrology (and I'm extremely into metaphysics), but I had no idea what she meant, so I did what any person would do—I Googled.

Apparently, Saturn takes approximately 29.5 years to complete one full orbit around the Sun, so from the age of about 27-30, Saturn will return to the same zodiac sign it was in when you were born. This return causes a cosmic shift in your personal life, which forces you to acknowledge the recurring lessons in your life so that you may be able to finally heed its message and move forward. Well, damn.

This was around the time that I realized my Dad's departure from my life took a much bigger toll on me than I'd accepted, and I was faced with the glaring conclusion that the lack of healthy love in my life was due to the fact that I didn't love myself. I tried to fake it, but my desperation to be accepted and valued could be sensed from a mile away. I knew if I wanted to attract a certain type of love in my life, I had to become that love myself. So, I did my best to practice self-love and self-care, but it wasn't easy, because I also realized that I treated myself worse than anybody else had treated me. I was so cruel to the girl staring back at me in the mirror, and she didn't deserve that. I had a lot of inner damage that needed resolution.

I started to write love letters to myself every morning, detailing bits about myself that I admired and reread them whenever I felt down. I continued with yoga and got deeper into my meditation to become grounded and remember that I'm never in this alone. I made sure to do at least a few things a week that made me happy, whether that was visiting my favorite used bookstore and getting lost in a new story or just listening to loud music for hours. I tried to catch myself in negative self-talk, and made an effort to stop speaking harmful words to myself. I no longer felt bad for wanting to spend more time alone, but made sure not to drown in my solitude too much, because spending time with people who love you is important, too. I took risks, I said yes to whatever opportunities came to me, I did things that scared me and

I allowed myself the freedom to get to know myself all over again without the filter of my inner critic.

And whaddya know? I really liked this woman.

Of course, there are still days that are harder than others—days when I look in the mirror and cringe, wishing I was just a touch skinnier or had clearer skin or didn't have dark circles or...you name it. There are also plenty of days when I wonder what the fuck I'm doing-am I on the right path? Am I screwing everything up? Do I even know what I really want?

I don't allow myself to spend too much time there, because it's a downward spiral, but I'm human, so I'd be lying if I said it's all rainbows and butterflies every day.

However, during this time of self-reflection and holding myself accountable to my actions, I learned many things about myself that really blew my mind. Yes, of course I'll share them with you. Duh.

Lesson No. 1: The Struggle Myth: I realized that I bought into the struggle myth from a young age, and I needed to break free. The words "nothing worth having comes easy" took control of my life and frankly, I came to find out that those words are not absolute truth. In fact, it was a limiting belief.

Sure, hard work reaps benefits, but I kept looking at life as one big obstacle course and questioned the legitimacy of anything that came without a cost. A lover that doesn't cause heartache? A job that doesn't create stress? Financial gain that didn't require selling my soul or sacrificing all of my time? *Nah, that's not real life.*

While that mentality definitely sharpened my work ethic and determination, it also made it nearly impossible to feel deserving of anything unless I went through hell for it. I always felt like I had to prove myself. I had to earn everything that I wanted in my life, and maybe there's some truth to that, but it's also true that sometimes you're given gifts simply because they're yours to have.

You will surely face obstacles on your journey, but it's important to be able to decipher a hurdle from a wall. Sometimes what you're fighting for, or what you're working so hard to achieve, is not what's meant for you.

So how can you tell the difference? When the passion is gone. When the love is gone. When the only reason you're still fighting is to prove a point. I learned that the only struggle I really had to overcome to gain what's rightfully mine was the ability to receive and know that I deserve it. I didn't have to question every good thing that came into my life just because I didn't have to sacrifice my sanity for it. I deserve everything. I just had to truly believe it and stop standing in my own damn way.

Lesson No. 2: The Dark Side of Being Selfless: Listen to me. Self-sacrifice is not an act of love if all you're actually doing is depleting yourself of the love you claim to give. Read that again.

For so long, my misconstrued connection between sacrifice and love cost me a lot of heartache. There is such a thing as being selfless to a fault, and when people would tell me that, I wouldn't understand what they were talking about. I always thought that being selfless was my way of showing love, but really I was just running myself into the ground for people in an effort to gain love back. I didn't realize that I was also subconsciously placing unrealistic expectations on them to do the same for me, and guess what? They never would. Instead, they'd choose to put themselves first, and I'd get pissed off, but not because I felt overlooked. I was pissed because I was never able to do that for myself. What initially felt like a curse of just loving people who couldn't love me back was actually a slap from the Universe to wake me up and tell me that I kept trying to manipulate the love in my life since I wouldn't learn how to love myself first. As with everything, living on the extreme ends of any spectrum is faulty. Being too selfless or too selfish is harmful. I needed to learn to find the sweet spot in the middle where balance lived.

Lesson No. 3: I'm Not the Center of the Universe: *Say what?* I know, right? As I mentioned, I always thought of myself as a very selfless person, and that's not a complete lie, but I also started to see that a lot of my actions were rooted in selfish desires. You experienced some of those throughout this book. I'd bend over backwards to show how great and loving I am, but secretly hope it'd be the trick to make them fall in love with me or expect them to do something just as amazing for me, and when they wouldn't, I'd throw a hissy fit when in actuality, it was my fault.

First of all, you can't expect people to approach every situation the same way you would, because as we've learned, everyone's different in how they perceive and receive love.

Secondly, in these instances, I had mentally placed myself as a priority in their lives, which clearly caused some misconstrued ideas of how things should go on my end, because I wasn't a priority for most of them.

I was always so scared of being left that I worried more about coming across as a person you couldn't live without than becoming the woman you loved to live with.

Lesson No. 4: I Had to Stop Playing the Victim: This one snuck up on me. Obviously, I'm artsy and poetic and brooding at times, so I have a dark side that comes to play, but whether it was subconscious or not, I was feeding that side a little too much. I've always said that being sad is easy. Allowing yourself to be happy is the challenge. I was the definition of that.

It was easy for me to date guys that never saw a future with me and to write about the heartbreak and to sulk in the sorrow that I'd voluntarily prolong for years, even though I knew I could've gotten over it much sooner. It was easy to blame exes or my father for my misfortune with relationships instead of facing the fact that I was choosing the wrong partners, ignoring red flags, dismissing boundaries and allowing certain behavior to disguise itself as love.

I knew better. I kept looking at my life as though everything was happening *to* me, when in actuality, I was allowing it all to happen. I was used to being the victim, and I had to get out of that.

Now, that's not to say that I willingly sought relationships that I knew would be bad for me from the jump. I wholeheartedly believed that a lot of these relationships came with pure intentions and potential of actual romance and commitment, but at some point, I'd always see the truth of the matter, and chose to stick around longer than I needed to.

Yes, I've endured abuse by people I trusted. Yes, I've harmed my physical body in hopes of overshadowing the emotional pain. Yes, I struggle with depression and anxiety. Yes, I've thought about taking my own life, and those thoughts never really go away completely.

But these setbacks don't define me. They're just experiences of my past, and each day I get to choose whether I want to become crippled by them or stack them up, brick by brick, so I can reach heights I never thought possible.

Lesson No. 5: Get Out of Your Story: Many of us are aware of The Law of Attraction (like energy attracts like energy), however, there's more to it than that. Your energy also attracts those who will complement your story, which means that whatever "role" you've chosen to fulfill, you will attract those who will play the right part to aid in continuing the role you've given yourself.

In my case, I realized that I kept feeding into my story, which was basically this:

I'm just some hopeless romantic who always gets the shitty end of the stick with love, because my father was emotionally absent and never really cared about me, so I chase after every emotionally unavailable man I can find in hopes that he'll love me back to health.

That was my story and there was some truth to it, because I stuck to my role for years and never dared to deviate from the script I had in my head of how things would unravel. So, of course I attracted people into my life that would help keep that narrative true. I was so deep in it, that I didn't even realize what I was doing. I kept mistaking attachment as love (and the lack of attachment as no love) and toxicity as passion. In order for me to attract different people, I had to be different. I had to fire myself from this horrible role that I took on without question for so long.

It was time for a new story. A better story.

I decided I wanted to let go of every unhealthy pattern, behavior and belief that I used as a crutch so that I could become a different woman. Is that easy? Hell no. Does the temptation to fall back into my comfortable, unhealthy behavior creep up? Absolutely. Will this self-work ever end? Probably not.

Should I still try every single day? Fuck yes.

Regardless of where you're at in your journey, if nothing else, please remember this—don't let your past or those who hurt you ever make you question if love is real. It's the only thing that's real, and it's everywhere. I see it with my friends who confess their love to one another, with my 63-year-old neighbor who decided to marry his high school sweetheart after 45 years apart, with the 95-year-old couple who sat in front of me in the theatre, with friends, family and even strangers who cross my path, because you don't find love. You *are* love.

The longest relationship any of us will ever have is the one we have with ourselves. So why don't we feed it with as much love, respect and loyalty as we do the other relationships in our lives? I always thought putting myself out on a limb for everyone I cared for was how I show my love, but I was wrong. The best way to show love is to become so completely inundated with love on my own, that my love spills over and touches everyone around me.

Forgiveness is the first step to loving unconditionally. Don't wait for the apology that you may never get or continue this game of, "But, do they deserve my forgiveness?" Maybe they don't, but *you* deserve some peace, don't you think? Forgiving those who've hurt you helps rid yourself of the anguish that you've been holding onto inside. And it doesn't have to be some elaborate gesture or dramatic conversation. All you have to do is make that shift consciously, and everything else will fall into place.

And while you're out here forgiving people, don't forget to forgive yourself, because we've all done things to ourselves that wasn't beneficial, but the silver lining is that we always have the opportunity to make it right again. Sneak a smile when you wake up in the morning, kiss the backs of your hands, admire the human being staring back at you in the mirror. Remember to give yourself the same patience, grace and healing that you so easily offer others. And never, ever forget, that the greatest love of all is already inside of you.

I forgive you. I forgive me. I hope you can forgive me, too.

I am a firm believer that the obstacles I've faced throughout my life are what helped mold me into the woman today, and while I am always a work in progress, I can say without a shadow of a doubt that I am proud of the person I have become. I can't be certain that I would be this person had I not experienced these situations (I probably wouldn't even be writing this book), so I have accepted all the baggage and weight that has been carried with me over the years, but it was time to let that shit go. You feel me?

Although I fully embrace every disillusioned relationship, every failed attempt at love and every moment of self-inflicted pain, because each circumstance was riddled with lessons that were necessary to my growth, I also had to learn that I don't need to sacrifice my mental and emotional health for the sake of learning a lesson.

I had to release this attachment I had to the old karmic paradigm of feeling that these lessons and the pain were necessary, and that the punishment was deserved. I don't need to manifest my fears to learn from them.

Once that message became clear, I started to shed all the layers of doubt, guilt, pain, heartbreak and anger, and I made it my mission to turn tragedy into triumph, because my happiness and well-being is *my* responsibility.

I share my journey with you, not because I think my story is *so* important that it must be told to the masses, but because I've experienced both sides of the spectrum. I am living proof that you can emerge from the deep-end of darkness back to the light. All you have to do is make a decision and stay committed.

So, with that said, are you ready to let shit go?

10

THE ONE ABOUT YOU

YOU'VE READ MY STORY, YOU KNOW MY STRUGGLE

YOU SAW HOW HARD IT IS TO FEEL LOVE WHEN YOU DON'T EVEN LOVE YOU

YOU MET MY FLAWS AND ALL MY DIRTY SECRETS, TOO

YOU SAW WHAT HAPPENS WHEN YOU OWN WHATEVER YOU WENT THROUGH

SO NOW IT'S YOUR TURN TO TAKE EVERYTHING YOU KNOW

AND GIVE YOURSELF PERMISSION TO LET THAT SHIT GO

The next few pages are for you to begin your journey of freeing yourself from whatever you feel is holding you down. I've provided some introspective questions as well as three writing prompts to help lead you.

Here's what a lot of people don't tell you, because then they can't make money off you—you already have all the answers you've been searching for. People may help lead you in the right direction, but no one is going to be able to hand you the magical solution to the inner peace that you've been seeking. You have to do that for you. You just have to dig a little deeper.

I hope these pages provide you with the same safety that they've given me, and I hope you remember to always look for the light in every dark moment, because it's there waiting to embrace you.

REFLECT

What does love mean to you? How do you show it? How do you receive it?

What are your top three values? How present are they in your life?

How are you showing up in the world?

What does a healthy, loving relationship look like to you?

THE CONVERSATION
I NEVER HAD

Are you lacking closure in a certain situation? Is there heaviness on your mind or in your heart over words left unsaid? Leave them here. Write the conversation that never came to be to free yourself of the weight that it leaves.

Turning Tragedy
Into Triumph

Everything we experience is either a blessing or a lesson. Explore that. Think of a painful experience that you've had and relive it here on the page, but this time, make sure to note the lessons that sprung from it. What did you learn? Why do you think this happened? What will you take away from it?

DEAR ME

Write a love letter to yourself. Highlight the things about yourself that you admire, the obstacles that you're proud of overcoming, the moments that tested you. Forgive yourself for your moments of doubt and weakness. Be gentle with yourself. Once you're done, sign it with, "I love you [name]," and read the letter aloud to yourself.

"I FORGIVE EVERYTHING AND EVERYONE, INCLUDING YOU, EVEN THOUGH I DON'T KNOW WHAT CRIME YOU HAVE COMMITTED.

I FORGIVE YOU BECAUSE I LOVE YOU AND BECAUSE YOU DON'T LOVE ME,

I FORGIVE YOU BECAUSE YOU HELP ME STAY CLOSE TO MY DEVIL, EVEN THOUGH I HAVEN'T THOUGHT OF HIM FOR YEARS.

I FORGIVE YOU BECAUSE YOU REJECT ME AND MY POWERS ARE WASTED,

I FORGIVE YOU BECAUSE YOU DON'T UNDERSTAND WHO I AM OR WHAT I AM DOING HERE.

I FORGIVE YOU AND THE DEVIL WHO TOUCHED MY BODY BEFORE I EVEN KNEW WHAT LIFE WAS ABOUT.

HE TOUCHED MY BODY, BUT DISTORTED MY SOUL.

I FREE MYSELF FROM HATRED THROUGH FORGIVENESS AND LOVE.

I UNDERSTAND THAT SUFFERING, WHEN IT CANNOT BE AVOIDED, IS HERE TO HELP ME ON MY WAY TO GLORY.

I UNDERSTAND THAT EVERYTHING IS CONNECTED, THAT ALL ROADS MEET, AND ALL RIVERS FLOW INTO THE SAME SEA.

That is why I am, at this moment, an instrument of forgiveness, forgiveness for crimes that were committed; one crime I know about, the other I do not.

I forgive the tears I was made to shed,

I forgive the pain and the disappointments,

I forgive the betrayals and the lies,

I forgive the slanders and intrigues,

I forgive the hatred and the persecution,

I forgive the blows that hurt me,

I forgive the wrecked dreams,

I forgive the still-born hopes,

I forgive the hostility and jealousy,

I forgive the indifference and ill will,

I forgive the injustice carried out in the name of justice,

I forgive the anger and the cruelty,

I forgive the neglect and the contempt

I forgive the world and all its evils.

I also forgive myself.

May the misfortunes of the past no longer weigh on my heart.

Instead of pain and resentment, I choose understanding and compassion.

Instead of rebellion, I choose the music from my violin.

Instead of vengeance, I choose victory.

I will be capable of loving regardless of whether I am loved in return,

Of giving even when I have nothing,

Of working happily even in the midst of difficulties,

Of holding out my hands even when utterly alone and abandoned,

Of drying my tears even while I weep,

Of believing even when no one believes in me.

So it is. So it will be."

—Aleph, Paulo Coelho

ABOUT THE AUTHOR

Bruna Nessif, an advocate for personal development & a self-proclaimed *hopeful* romantic, is the founder of the website The Problem With Dating, a multimedia platform that provides entertaining yet thoughtful pieces about love, dating, self-reflection & spiritual growth.

Bruna's written work has been featured on multiple publications, including *E! News, Playboy, Huffington Post, Cosmopolitan, Esquire* and *Bravo*.

She is currently enrolled in the Institute of Professional Excellence in Coaching to become a certified and accredited life coach for high conscious living, specializing in self-love and relationships. Additionally, she has been studying energy work & is continuing her journey to becoming a master reiki healer.

Made in the USA
Middletown, DE
21 January 2021

32139442R00166